ROYAL F

ROYAL SCANDAL

HOW SCANDAL THREATENS
A THOUSAND YEARS OF
BRITISH SOVEREIGNTY

ROLAND GOUGH

THE DUNWICH PRESS

CONTENTS

CHAPTER ONE:
A TICKING BOMB IN BUCKINGHAM PALACE

You read it here first: now that Queen Elizabeth II has passed away, the British Monarchy is about to be blown sky-high and vanish forever as an institution in the United Kingdom.

As Britain enters a new age, with a new king, as we shall see, Great Britain is no longer a 'united' kingdom. Nor is it willing to suffer so many members of the Royal Family being paid a fortune out of its work-overburdened and covid-weary taxpayers for very much longer. No royal position is safe – not even that of king. Profound change is imminent, and it will be dramatic. When regimes topple they go very fast. The modern world is unstable. As Yeats put it, 'Things fall apart'. And that is what the Royal Family is doing – and has been doing for a long time – falling apart, right before our eyes.

The speeches and actions of the new king Charles III have garnered a deal of sympathy since the death of his mother. But, make no mistake, he is fundamentally different to his predecessor in temperament, outlook and his approach to royal life – sufficiently so that huge swathes of the British Public are rapidly turning against him. Or, more accurately, are continuing to wax ever more critical and impatient with him as a person, and look to other means of providing a figurehead for the constitution of the United Kingdom.

A comment left below a YouTube Film about King Charles reads: *'If Soviet Russia can break up, every white-governed regime in Africa be overthrown, the Arab world go up in flames, the Chinese turn to overt capitalism, and a mob take over the Capitol building in Washington DC, then the British Monarchy should be quaking in its boots.'* [1]

He could be right. He *is* right. In these ever more politically volatile times, the Royal Family are more than a little nervous. And so they should be, with the younger generations of their 'subjects' in particular anxious about their futures and also hopping mad about the direction their country is taking.

The following questionnaire – conducted while the queen was alive – throws up some interesting answers. In fact *all* the answers are intriguing. The purpose of the survey was to discover the viewpoints of 'generation Z' youngsters, that is, British citizens born after 1995. The answers speak for themselves:

POLL OF YOUNG ADULTS AGED 14 -22

Q1. Do you support the Royal Family?
Yes 29%   No 63%

Q2. Do you think Prince Charles would make a good king?
Yes 13%   No 78%

Q3. Would you prefer an elected President rather than a monarch? Yes 55%   No 42%

Q4. Would Prince William make a good king?
Yes 59%   No 13%

Q5. Do the Royal Family receive too much of taxpayers' money?
Yes 93%   No 6%

Q6. Are there too many members of the Royal Family performing public duties?
Yes 74%   No 21%

Q7. Should Prince Andrew be removed from all public offices and have all his titles removed?

6

Yes 91%   No 5%

Q8. Should all royal residences be open to the public and tourists all year round?

Yes 57%   No 33%

Q9. Should the Royal Family make all their accounts open to public scrutiny

Yes 93%   No 4%

Q10. Should the royal Family pay tax on all of its income?

Yes 89%   No 8%

Q11. Should Camilla be granted the title of 'Queen Consort'?

Yes 16%   No 81%

Q12. Should William be made king when the Queen dies?

Yes 46%   No 34%

SOURCE: U-POLLS. POLL SAMPLE OF 1041 MIXED GROUP UK YOUNG CITIZENS, AGED 14 TO 22. POLLED JANUARY 1 TO FEB 28 2022

The writing is on the wall – or rather on the internet. The United Kingdom is undergoing something of a social revolution at present. In today's volatile 'WOKE' and celebrity-critical culture, old ideas and institutions are toppling like dominoes. And, when it comes to modern day 'cancel-culture', the British, led by a vanguard of disenchanted youth, are arguably the most trigger-happy assassins of famous folk anywhere in the world.

Let your mind drift back to one fateful day in January 2022 when the prime minister was cowering in his office after being lampooned and urged to quit office for holding a drinks office party during a lockdown. While Boris Johnson smarted from a press and social media onslaught, Buckingham Palace advisers were holding crisis talks about what to do about the sex-scandal hit Duke of York, Prince Andrew, after it became plain that he would have to defend himself in a trial in the USA – or else settle out of court for millions of dollars.

The scandal Prince Andrew was facing brought to a head the seething disaffection felt by a large proportion of the British public, a deep-seated unease at the bizarre and questionable behaviour of the Queen's favourite son.

The prospect of a trial, and the spectacle of Prince Andrew and his legal team floundering in their attempts to discredit his accuser, Virginia Giuffre, created a perfect storm on the platforms of social media. Meanwhile, the British Press took up the case of Ms Giuffre, and released a torrent of criticism aimed directly at the Duke of York.

But the country that had torn down statues of slave-owning dignitaries and voiced criticism at Winston Churchill's colonialist attitudes would not be content to lay heavily into Prince Andrew alone. No, it was about to turn on its biggest target to date, namely… the entire Royal Family.

In these rebellious times no-one is exempt from criticism. Even the Queen herself was openly criticised on social media platforms on occasion. This stemmed partly from disenchantment over the way that Buckingham Palace seemed to be protecting the allegedly wayward Prince Andrew. But other factors were also at play – for example, a deep-seated indignation that the Royal Family is sucking in and wasting vast sums of public money in a time of austerity. Furthermore, a simmering dissatisfaction of the enormous privileges enjoyed by 'the Royals' surfaces time and time again in social media posts.

This is not surprising. The British like their public figu[...]
be hard-working, incorruptible and seemingly approachabl[...]
an example set by the Queen, whom many thousands of Brits
saw close-up at garden parties or while performing her public
duties – at least in her younger days. 'Her Majesty' was widely
praised for her work ethic, inscrutability and highly moral
standards of life.

The antithesis, so far as the public are concerned, might be
Prince Andrew, perceived as haughty, aloof and domineering.
This is reflected in the following popularity poll, the public
being asked to say whether they approve or disapprove of each
member of the Royal Family. Again, it was conducted in the last
months of Queen Elizabeth's reign:

	Approve	Disapprove
The Queen	85%	5%
William, Duke of Cambridge	73%	11%
Kate, Duchess of Cambridge	72%	8%
Anne, Princess Royal	48%	21%
Edward, Duke of Wessex	39%	32%
Meghan, Duchess of Sussex	38%	36%
Sophie, Duchess of Wessex	35%	41%
Prince Harry, Duke of Sussex	35%	40%
Princes Charles	29%	52%
Princess Eugenie	21%	56%
Princess Beatrice	20%	49%
Camilla, Duchess of Cornwall	19%	59%
Prince Andrew	3%	87%

SOURCE: U-POLLS, SAMPLE 928 UK CITIZENS May. 2022

As can be seen, Prince Andrew does not merely come last.

re to be believed, the lame duck of the royal
link in the royal chain of command has always
g to the British press, the very epitome of
er-consumption, unearned privileges and pig-
nce. His life of luxury spent at Buckingham
Palace and other royal residences has been singled out for
ridicule more than that of any other 'Royal'. Prince Andrew, the
Queen's second son, was once lauded as a Falklands War hero –
as a helicopter pilot he was famously used to divert Exocet
missiles from his Aircraft Carrier Hermes. But, though the
Argentines couldn't touch him, the scandal-hit Duke has
latterly found himself shot down in flames by the more hard-
hitting elements of the British and world press.

Long before the death of Queen Elizabeth, the public's
attitude toward Prince Andrew was driving a huge wedge of
mistrust between the Royal Family and the 'common' people of
Great Britain.

Once lost, respect, like true love, is impossible to retrieve or
rekindle. And, unfortunately, events have conspired to fatally
wound the love affair between the British populace and their
royal head of state. After all, Prince Andrew is brother to the
new king. Efforts to distance King Charles and Prince William
from the Prince are rather too late, the damage having already
been done. In the years before the passing of the late Queen,
social media was full of posts highly critical of how Andrew
continued to live in Buckingham Palace and was, allegedly,
trying to rehabilitate himself into public life and confidence.

This disenchantment did not begin, but did become more
shrill and widespread when Virginia Giuffre made it plain she
intended to take Andrew to court in the USA on charges

relating to her being trafficked for sex at the age of seventeen, and allegedly forced into having relations with the Prince by the billionaire paedophile Jeffrey Epstein.

A veritable explosion of social media posts hostile to Prince Andrew began to circulate on Twitter. The furore was simultaneously taken up by the British press.

Newspapers, both the paper version and the online editions, have always had a crucial role in influencing public opinion on Shakespeare's 'sceptred isle'. Here is a selection of the explosive flak that landed all around Prince Andrew (and Buckingham Palace) on one single day, 13 January 2022.

From the most widely sold paper, THE SUN comes:

DUKE OF HAZARD ANDREW BREAKS COVER AT WINDSOR AFTER LOSING BATTLE TO AVOID SEX TRIAL

THE DAILY MAIL, beloved rag of the middle classes rants:

IDIOT ANDREW IS OUT OF OPTIONS... THE ONLY THING HE CAN DO IS AVOID HUMILIATING HIS MOTHER IN COURT IS TO PAY OFF HIS SEX ACCUSER AND VANISH FOREVER FROM BRITISH LIFE.

The illustrious TELEGRAPH booms:

TIME TO PAY UP – ANDREW RISKS HUMILIATION IN COURT

The prestigious THE TIMES laments:

ANDREW'S ACCUSER DETERMINED TO GO TO TRIAL

The pro-Royal Family DAILY EXPRESS headlines:

PRINCE ANDREW LIVE – QUEEN URGED TO AXE ALL MILITARY TITLES – 152 ANGRY VETERANS SIGN LETTER

And finally the DAILY STAR, beloved rag of the lower orders cries out:

PRINCE ANDREW CASE TO DESTROY PALACE'S 'IRON CURTAIN OF SECRECY' AS MEGHAN MAY TESTIFY

As it turned out, Meghan Markle testifying against fellow 'royal' Prince Andrew never happened, though the damaging suggestion of royal infighting did no favours to the reputation of either Meghan or Andrew.

But how did all this press-borne hostility come about? Is it really true to say that Prince Andrew brought all this on himself? Or was he just the victim of some kind of 'sting' designed to bring him down? While Andrew is widely regarded in Britain as something of a pompous idiot, it is a far cry from being guilty of sex crimes involving an underage girl, as many of the social media posts alleged. The Prince protested his innocence, and vowed to fight the allegations. But, alas, the more information that came to light, the more he was lambasted and singled out for a frenzy of media attention. His royal goose was already cooked – for, as we shall soon see, with friends like JEFFREY EPSTEIN and GHISLAINE MAXWELL, who would ever need enemies?

CHAPTER TWO:
CONSPIRACY, SUICIDE AND SHAME:
AMERICAN S**T HITS BRITISH FAN

The question many asked was whether Prince Andrew really did sleep with women – or rather, young girls – trafficked around the world by Jeffrey Epstein and Ghislaine Maxwell. Certainly, the international press seemed to think so. Social media is still rife with accusations and condemnations of the beleaguered prince. But in order to get to the bottom of all this, it is necessary to take a look at what exactly Prince Andrew, the Duke of York, has been accused of, and who has been doing the accusing.

Serious allegations were levelled at him by Virginia Giuffre, formerly Virginia Roberts, a US citizen now residing in Australia, but filing charges via the courts of New York. Her principal lawyer is David Boise, who repeated many times that 'Virginia Giuffre is not interested in purely financial settlement with Prince Andrew'. This means that she would not spare Prince Andrew the ordeal of court by accepting a big financial settlement unless Andrew publicly apologised, or admitted to some degree of wrongdoing.

An admission or apology, however, would be virtually impossible for him, as this would imply he was guilty of her allegations and so render him liable to further prosecutions both in the USA and in Great Britain, for reasons that shall be made plain later in this book. But what exactly was the prince (according to Ms Giuffre) supposed to be guilty of doing in the first place?

The basis of her civil case was a series of allegations that Andrew had sexual relations with her on three separate occasions. The places were Jeffrey Epstein's houses in New York, the U.S. Virgin Islands and in London. The case is THIS:

Giuffre alleges that Prince Andrew, the Duke of York had sex with her when she was a minor (aged 17) and that she was forced to do so as a trafficked victim of the late billionaire-paedophile Jeffrey Epstein and his accomplice Ghislaine Maxwell.

The Duke has categorically denied having sex with Giuffre. She, however, signed statements under oath in US courts alleging that Andrew had sex with her on three times in three separate locations. In her civil legal case Giuffre also alleged that the late financier Jeffrey Epstein trafficked her and forced her to have sexual relations with his friends or with whomsoever he told her, including Prince Andrew – who she alleges was aware of her age at that time. Being only 17, she fell below the age of consent in Florida and United States Virgin Islands, where two of the alleged offences took place.

Age notwithstanding, as a victim of sex trafficking, any contact of a sexual nature with Virginia Giuffre would render the perpetrator guilty of a felony.

She alleges the Prince sexually abused her at Epstein's private island in the US Virgin Islands, at his mansion in Manhattan and at his former girlfriend Ghislaine Maxwell's home in London. Virginia Giuffre's lawyers allege he 'committed sexual assault and battery' upon her when she was a teenager. Unsurprisingly, Andrew vehemently denies the allegations.

In claims made prior to the formal filing her lawsuit, Giuffre alleges that she was conveyed by Epstein to London, where she was introduced to Prince Andrew. There, she said, she was coerced into doing whatever he wished. In a BBC interview broadcast in 2019, Giuffre alleged she had been taken to Tramp nightclub where Andrew asked her to dance and was 'sweating all over me.'

After dancing at a nightclub with Epstein, Maxwell and the Prince she said they returned to Ghislaine Maxwell's house in Belgravia, an expensive area of London, where she had to have sex with the prince. She was allegedly paid $15,000.

The Scottish comedian Frankie Boyle said that this proves the story was untrue – no woman would agree to such an ordeal for only $15,000!

Joking aside, this gruesome story, and her stating that she in fact had to endure sexual encounters with Andrew three times in three separate houses owned by Epstein is of course denied by Andrew.

Returning to the subject of the nightclub where Giuffre says she was taken by the prince, the location is most curious. Tramp is a nightclub famed for its discretion. Paparazzi and autograph hunters are banned. Here the rich and famous can drink, dance and cavort to their hearts content with little risk to their privacy. Tramp was the place Prince Andrew chose for his first date with former girlfriend Koo Stark. In later years, Andrew and Sarah Ferguson attended regularly. If Giuffre in fact made up her story, she had certainly done some homework before creating a narrative.

Giuffre's sworn statements regarding all three of these alleged sexual encounters are serious stuff for Andrew. Under

English law the age of consent is sixteen, but having sex with a trafficked person is a criminal offence, with penalties upon conviction that might include a lengthy time in prison.

Giuffre said she also encountered Prince Andrew, twice, in the USA. In the city of New York, alleged scene of one of these meetings, the age of consent is 17. But participating in human trafficking of a minor (under 18) is a Class B felony and carries a maximum sentence of 25 years in prison. This is classified as a strict liability offense. Whether the trafficker had knowledge the victim was minor is irrelevant and not a defense. There are related offenses of Kidnap (Class A felony), Unlawful Imprisonment (Class A misdemeanor), Custodial Interference (class A misdemeanor) and Promoting Prostitution (class C or D felony).

Serious punishments indeed, and in the US Virgin Islands there are equally stringent laws, with possibly greater penalties for sex traffickers and those associated with them. This includes individuals having sexual relations with enslaved victims, and 'ignorance of the fact' is no defense. At the time of writing this, the US Virgin Islands' Attorney General is filing and pursuing charges against the Epstein Estate with a view to prosecuting his associates, fining or imprisoning them, seizing assets from Epstein's trust funds and companies, amongst other measures.

Who knows what the investigators will turn up as they interview victim after victim, and interrogate ex-staff and former employees of the paedophile. They are also reportedly ploughing through tons of incriminating documents and testimonies. Associates of Jeffrey Epstein who committed an offence in the Virgin Islands should be feeling rather nervous, not to mention terrified, at what might be discovered.

As for Prince Andrew, the trouble is, that instead of initially agreeing to fight it out in court and denying Virginia Giuffre's allegations, Andrew's lawyers decided to hide behind the protection of the $500,000 legal settlement of 2009 agreed by Epstein for abusing Giuffre, which contained an expansive release clause shielding 'other potential defendants' from civil liability.

Think of it: a British prince hiding behind the deceased Jeffrey Epstein's highly suspect and deplorable 2009 legal agreement, a so-called 'sweetheart deal' that gave the paedophile only 18 months jail time on, though he was freed after only 13 months.

It was foreseeable that this deplorable tactic should come to nought. Epstein had been dealing with the state of Florida, while Giuffre's lawyers were constructing a civil case against Prince Andrew in New York. Judge Kaplan of Southern New York made the historic ruling that Epstein's deal 'did not stand' and that the trial must go ahead.

Before this, it was said that the Duke of York's lawyers had been very evasive to avoid Giuffre having her day in court. Her representatives, reportedly, were unable to get responses to their questions, nor serve legal papers on the prince in any of his residences.

There were embarrassing scenes on British and world TV and media outlets on 16 November 2019, five months after Epstein's death, when Geoffrey Berman, US Attorney for the Southern District of New York, publicly accused Prince Andrew's lawyers of avoiding and delaying his investigations. He told the media at a press conference:

'Now ordinarily our office doesn't comment on whether an

17

individual co-operates or doesn't co-operate with our investigation. However, in Prince Andrew's case, he publically offered, indeed in a press release offered to co-operate with law enforcers investigating the crimes committed by Jeffrey Epstein and his co-conspirators, so I think in that context it's fair for people to know whether Prince Andrew has followed through with that public commitment. So let me say that the Southern District of New York and the FBI have contacted Prince Andrew's attorneys and requested to interview Prince Andrew and [up to the] present Prince Andrew has provided zero co-operation.

'The original charges against Prince Andrew contained a conspiracy charge and we alleged that there were conspirators involved and Jeffrey Epstein couldn't have done what he did without the assistance of others and I can assure you that our investigation is moving forward.'

In other words, he was still busily engaged in the process of investigating Andrew's possible conduct regarding Virginia Giuffre. But by March 2021 Berman, growing impatient and realizing he was unlikely to get any assistance, said Prince Andrew's team had shut the door on co-operation.

Time and again Andrew's representatives reportedly failed to respond to the Department of Justice's requests, giving answers that suggested the Americans were to blame for the delays to procedures. Berman was incensed enough to say to the international media:

'Today Prince Andrew has yet again sought to falsely portray himself to the public as eager and willing to co-operate... However, Prince Andrew has not given an interview to federal authorities, and has repeatedly declined our request to schedule

such an interview, and nearly four months ago informed us unequivocally - through the very same counsel who issued today's release - that he would not come in for such an interview. If Prince Andrew is, in fact, serious about co-operating with the ongoing federal investigation, our doors remain open, and we await word of when we should expect him.'

The duke's lawyers made no formal reply, but gave a press statement through a 'source' stating:

'This is the third time Berman has breached his own confidentiality rules, further diminishing our trust in the Department of Justice's willingness to play a straight bat. It's frankly bewildering.'

The expression to play 'a straight bat' is an expression from cricket, and suggests conducting oneself with directness, honesty and integrity. But this was a case of the pot calling the kettle black! Andrew's team were suggesting the Department of Justice was somehow the evasive party here.

However, reporters, journalists and political commentators were unanimous in putting the blame squarely on Prince Andrew's lawyers and advisors. As for the campaign of delay waged against the Department of Justice, the (British) Telegraph later said:

'A Knight of the Most Noble Order of the Garter does not refuse to co-operate with the FBI in a criminal investigation or fail to give a full version of what he knows under oath. Nor does he scuttle about the country, playing an embarrassing game of hide and seek, to avoid having legal papers served on him.' [2]

The American press were also incensed and appalled by the delays and obstacles they said Andrew's team were using to evade a showdown at trial. And no wonder. Shortly after his infamous BBC Newsnight TV interview was broadcast on 16 November 2019, Prince Andrew said he was 'willing to help any appropriate US law enforcement agency' with their investigations. This was said by the American media to be nothing more than empty words and 'spin' to mollify and convince the British and American public that the Prince was willing to co-operate when really his team's strategy was to avoid, side-step or simply ignore requests for information. It was said that Andrew would 'do anything' rather than testify before a court, never mind voluntarily giving a deposition before American lawyers.

Was he so frightened and lacking in faith of the American legal system that he feared he would somehow be unfairly treated? Or was it that he really did have terrible secrets to hide that must not, under any circumstances come under the scrutiny of justice, and the attention of the British, American and even world public opinion? Should an innocent man with the legal resources of the British Crown really be so terrified of one young American woman seeking to have her day in court? That the prince's legal team were stonewalling the US department of justices' attempts to get him to respond seem undeniable. In January 2020, Mr Berman re-iterated once more that the prince had provided 'zero co-operation'. Later in March 2020 he stated Andrew had 'completely shut the door' on assisting his enquiries.

By way of reply, Prince Andrew's legal team tried to imply they were willing to take part in the legal process: 'The Duke of York,' they said, 'has on at least three occasions this year offered his assistance as a witness to the US Department of

Justice. Unfortunately, the Department of Justice has reacted to the first two offers by breaching their own confidentiality rules and claiming that the duke has offered zero co-operation. In doing so, they are perhaps seeking publicity rather than accepting the assistance proffered.'

Unknown to the British public, at least at first, that same day the Department of Justice had issued a formal request to speak to the prince as part of its Epstein inquiry by submitting a mutual legal assistance (MLA) request to the UK Home Office.

A MLA request ensured that if Prince Andrew did not voluntarily respond, he could be called to a UK court to answer questions. Prince Andrew's team, even if relieved the document was at least kept secret from the public, knew that this ticking bomb would soon have to be dealt with.

But alas, before they could act, the MLA was leaked to the British press. The duke's lawyers were reportedly furious. [3] The very point of their avoiding American courts and legal wrangling was to keep the Press and public from savaging the prince. Now it seemed the Americans acting on behalf of Giuffre had Andrew's team check-mated.

For, if the British courts had ordered Prince Andrew to make a sworn statement outlining his defense, the trial would effectively have begun. With Giuffre and the witnesses testifying on her behalf willing to give contrary evidence to Prince Andrew, much of his evidence would have been opposed, thus heightening the stakes.

With the world's attention on Prince Andrew, the trust and faith the British people have in the Royal Family was greatly shaken. The brother of the future King Charles III seemed to be behaving in a wholly dishonourable and disreputable fashion. The question being asked was *when* would Prince Andrew actually stand his ground and defend himself?

Because it was perceived the Prince's legal team had began stonewalling and avoiding having legal papers served on him, suspicions everywhere – especially in Britain – were riding even higher than before that this son of Queen Elizabeth had something to hide. Surely, though, he would fight it out. Wouldn't he?

After an hour or two of stunned silence, Prince Andrew's lawyers' response to the potentially disastrous MLA was announced. His lawyers called it 'disappointing' – an example of British understatement if ever there was one.

'The Duke of York is not a target of the Department of Justice's investigation,' they said, 'and has recently repeated his willingness to provide a witness statement'.

But, so far as Virginia Giuffre was concerned, Prince Andrew *was* a target of investigation. Then, once again, Andrew's lawyers decided to close ranks and await events, while the inevitable clamour of the popular press castigated the prince's tactics of avoiding an open trial.

There was an even more ominous and deadly deluge of criticism from those using the dreaded social media... and the traffic of harsh messages turned out to be almost unanimously in support of Virginia Giuffre, and furious at the way the prince's lawyers were conducting their campaign.

As one tweet stated, regarding the case:

'Surely the mighty Prince Andrew can't be afraid of facing Virginia Roberts-Giuffre in a fair and open trial? I mean, if he really is innocent, what's the f***'s he got to lose?'

Then, finally, things came to a head: an event in the USA made it impossible for the prince and his team to stall any longer. The day of final reckoning had finally arrived...

CHAPTER THREE:
THE TRIAL IS ANNOUNCED AND THE PRINCE GETS CANCELLED – BY HIS MOTHER!

On 12 January 2022 at about 2pm in the afternoon (British time) Prince Andrew's plight grew even worse: the verdict of Judge Lewis A Kaplan of the United States District Court for the Southern District of New York was that the civil trial must go ahead.

In a 46 page document he outlined his decision to dismiss Prince Andrew's lawsuit that had sought to avoid a trial. This meant the case against Prince Andrew would be heard in the late summer or fall of 2022 – unless the Princes' lawyers moved to settle the matter out of court, which would inevitably mean the payment of a multi-million dollar sum to Ms Giuffre.

Her lawyer, David Boies, spoke to reporters: 'She looks forward to a judicial determination of the merits of those claims.' Giuffre added that she was very pleased that the next stage of the process could now go ahead. This would involve the giving of depositions (verbal evidence given under oath in the form of questions submitted and answered by both parties). Federal Judge Kaplan set things in motion for a trial after dismissing Prince Andrew's assertion that the case against him was 'legally insufficient' and therefore could not be grounds for a full court trial. Furthermore, he ruled that Epstein's 2009 settlement made in Florida 'cannot be said to benefit Prince Andrew'. He also stated that his ruling had not considered the 'defendant's efforts to cast doubt on the truth of Ms Giuffre's allegations, even though his efforts would be permissible at trial'.

In addition, 'In a similar vein and for similar reasons, it is not open to the court now to decide, as a matter of fact, just what the parties to the release in the 2009 settlement agreement signed by Ms Giuffre and Jeffrey Epstein actually meant.'

He went on: 'Ms. Giuffre's complaint is neither 'unintelligible' nor 'vague' nor 'ambiguous'. He said that 'It alleges discrete incidents of sexual abuse in particular circumstances at three identifiable locations. It identifies to whom it attributes that sexual abuse.' In other words, the case of Virginia Giuffre was plausible, and the grounds for dismissing it were not.

The long and the short of all this is that Andrew would now face the music in court... or somehow persuade Giuffre to settle for a large out-of-court settlement.

While it was possible Prince Andrew's legal team might launch an appeal against Judge Kaplan's decision, it was unlikely to succeed, given that no new evidence or grounds to dismiss the ruling were forthcoming. Furthermore, the wording of Kaplan's judgement implied that an appeal would not be looked upon favourably, and would in all likelihood be thrown out.

Therefore, the next stage, would now forge ahead, with lawyers for Andrew and Virginia Giuffre and Prince Andrew testing each other's stories by deposition. This meant that both parties could provide detailed personal evidence that would be pored over for weaknesses, inconsistencies, and of course, potential lies. And by autumn of 2022 a civil trial would enable Ms Giuffre's lawyers to put her allegations directly to the prince.

After these bombshells, social media sites grew red-hot with criticism of Prince Andrew, and the Great British Press roared into action, spewing forth the headlines reproduced in chapter one of this book.

And it did not help the reputation of the Royal Family in general that Andrew appeared, according to the Press, to be conducting matters from Buckingham Palace itself, the very centre and heart of British Royalty.

Even before Prince Andrew's legal team and personal advisers could react to the media storm, the higher echelons at Buckingham Palace reacted in stunning fashion, and announced that the prince had lost most of his military titles. The statement issued from Buckingham Palace 'with the Queen's approval and agreement' suggested Her Majesty agreed to the measures, but that the orders did not originate from her. The media speculated that Prince Charles (as he was then titled) and Prince William were instrumental in the moves against Andrew, though there has never been any confirmation of this.

In one day, Andrew was ignominiously stripped of the following ranks:

Colonel of the prestigious Grenadier Guards
Colonel-in-chief of the Royal Lancers (Queen Elizabeth's Own)
Colonel-in-chief of the Yorkshire Regiment
Honorary air commodore of RAF Lossiemouth
Colonel-in-chief of the Royal Irish Regiment
Colonel-in-chief of the Small Arms School Corps
Royal colonel of the Royal Highland Fusiliers

Royal colonel of the Royal Regiment of Scotland
Commodore-in-chief of the Fleet Air Arm

The duke was also been stripped of several overseas honorary roles including:

Colonel-in-chief of the Royal New Zealand Army Logistic Regiment
Colonel-in-chief of the Princess Louise Fusiliers of Canada
Colonel-in-chief of the Royal Highland Fusiliers of Canada
Colonel-in-chief of the Queen's York Rangers.

His service rank of Vice-Admiral was retained, leaving him free to wear at least one uniform on formal occasions. His standing in the armed forces had already been questioned in the newspapers, since even though he had left the armed forces, he had nevertheless been promoted in 2015 to the rank of Vice-Admiral. This occurred on his 55th birthday, and he was reportedly due to be promoted to full Admiral on his 60th birthday in 2020, but 'requested' to defer this after stepping back from public duties. However, with the removal of so many of his honorary titles the message was now clear – the Duke of York was no longer considered a suitable person for the rank of Colonel-in-Chief of an army regiment. (Most of the charities he headed or championed also sought to drop him with unseemly haste, but more of this later).

By stripping the Duke of York of his military titles, Buckingham Palace hoped to contain the fall-out from Prince Andrew's disastrous plummet from grace. But would this damage limitation actually work?

The Prince Andrew Fan Club site on Facebook revealed some clues with posts such as:

'Prince Andrew is innocent, Everyone knows that.' Ben M

And the next one –

'More trouble for the House of Windsor. Can't wait for more s**t to come out and nail this arrogant pompous nonce. Paul C.

There are numerous other anti-Prince Andrew posts trolling this once exclusively pro-Duke of York forum.

A few years ago it would have been unthinkable that a Royal Prince might be so shamed. But it was also unthinkable that a certain section of Britain's population might clamour for the removal of Winston Churchill's statue on the grounds of him being 'colonialist' and 'racist'.

It was also never deemed possible that politicians, famous writers, university professors and even rock stars should have their reputations and livelihoods torn to shreds in the merciless piranha-pool of public opinion.

The question is, who is next for a public beheading? The Royal Family was already receiving much criticism at the hands of an angry and sceptical public, and it was not just Andrew who had riled the British masses. King Charles, known then as Prince Charles, had also already been receiving great criticism and was slipping into the shallow but deadly waters of a social media feeding frenzy before a greater scandal rocked him and his advisors working out of Clarence House on the Mall in London.

On 16 February 2022 the story broke that London's Metropolitan Police Force was launching an investigation into an alleged 'cash for honours' scandal. This was reportedly prompted by information forwarded in September 2021 by the anti-royalist 'Republic' organisation headed by their CEO Graham Smith.

The investigation began looking into allegations linking Prince Charles' 'Princes Foundation' with donations and offers of help from a Saudi national in return for honours and possible British citizenship.

The Prince's team have countered by stating that Prince Charles had no knowledge of the alleged offer of honours or British citizenship on the basis of donations to his charities.

One wonders what fresh horrors shall come to light and threaten the Royal Family's integrity and standing in the eyes of the already shocked British public, and whether the institution of Monarchy can remain intact after being rocked by a constant barrage of explosively bad news.

While the Queen Elizabeth lived, the British monarchy and constitution at least had a certain solidity due to its great age and past reputation for integrity and service to the nation. But with Charles now reigning as king, all eyes are turned on him. A penchant for talking to plants, and history of marketing expensive Duchy of Cornwall cookies may not be quite enough for the good folk of the united kingdom to continue to pay him homage.

The highly critical Republic group, are keen to point out how much taxpayers money is lavished on Royal Family members through sovereign grant payments, and by other means such as allowances, free accommodation and free travel.

They are dubious the public will be happy to pay the £3,00,000[4] King Charles will need just to pay the fuel bill on the 774 room Buckingham Palace. There are 22 other Royal Residences also to consider, with most members of the family having access to multiple homes. Meanwhile, as pensioners freeze for want of money to pay their fuel bills, businesses go bust in the post-covid economy, and the National Health Service struggles to deal with a backlog of hundreds of thousands of sick patients, will the British public tolerate the eccentric Prince Charles as the unelected head of the constitution?

His suitability has also been doubted by some because of his alleged love of penning letters of 'advice' to politicians, local authorities and individuals in various elected offices power. But more on him later.

First we need to return to the most unpopular member of the tribe, and see exactly why his legal case polarised public opinion so strongly against the once unassailable Royal Family.

If social media is to be believed, the Duke was not likely to be forgiven, given the predominantly critical tweets and messages posted. The 'Prince Andrew Fan Club' has had messages posted such as:

'How can someone set up a page worshipping a known child molester and possible paedophile? Andrew would be in prison now if the queen had not paid 12 million in bribe money to keep the nasty little pervert out of prison. She is as guilty as him and British people need to stand up and demand equal justice for everyone, not just those who can afford it.' Bob J

It is worth going a little deeper into this matter: the conduct of a senior Royal Family member, *and how he behaved over several decades without being reprimanded by his fellow Royals* – at least for a very long time – shows the institution of royalty in a very poor light. And some of the events and allegations that came to the public's attention are, if true, very shocking indeed.

CHAPTER FOUR:
A NIGHT TO REMEMBER: EPSTEIN, MAXWELL AND THE INFAMOUS PHOTOGRAPH

For twenty years Prince Andrew was an associate of Jeffrey Epstein. When the latter's crimes including paedophilia and sex trafficking were exposed, and Andrew did not break clean away from the billionaire, this did not go down well in Great Britain.

The press and media in general condemned him, yet he continued his association long after it was clear to the world that Epstein was a very sinister character.

The general feeling of the public in the United Kingdom was that Buckingham Palace as an institution supported Prince Andrew, come what may. By continuing to live in the Palace, and be involved in the public duties of a 'working' Royal, the prince unwittingly involved the other members of his family. His own unpopularity increased as the magnitude of the criminality of Jeffrey Epstein and Ghislaine Maxwell was shockingly revealed to the British public.

The hugeness of the mistake of visiting Epstein in December 2010 after it was crystal-clear what the billionaire was about cannot be over-emphasized. And despite Prince Andrew's protests that he had not been a close friend of Epstein, or Maxwell, the public made up its own mind.

Even before Andrew's disastrous BBC interview in November 2019, if there was one single thing that turned public opinion more strongly than ever in the United Kingdom, it was the famous photograph of him with his arm around Virginia Giuffre taken at Ghislaine Maxwell's house.

The image of Prince Andrew, Virginia Giuffre and Ghislaine Maxwell has been reproduced in newspapers and magazines across the globe. Andrew himself said that he had 'no recollection' of ever meeting Giuffre or of the picture being taken. Again, the British public made up their own minds about this, and Andrew was never given the benefit of the doubt.

I showed it to a retired British C.I.D. (Criminal Investigation Department) detective Robert Bird[5] for comments and analysis, and after several hours of professional scrutiny he came up with the following very telling observations:

BIRD: *'It's a fascinating but deeply troubling photograph. I've examined it over and over, and come to several conclusions assisted by what I've read about its context. I've listed them as follows...*

1. 'My first thoughts are that it's not a great quality image, a disposable Kodak or a cheap automatic or something similar. Was that because a cheap camera would look more innocuous and not raise Andrew's suspicions that he was being snapped in a compromising position? I wonder...

2. Virginia Giuffre's arm is not quite touching her side, showing the picture was taken quickly, and Prince Andrew seems ill-at-ease and tense, but reacting instinctively as one does to a camera and trying to smile. I reckon this was snapped before Prince Andrew had time to consider the picture's possible consequences for him and could offer any objection. Incidentally, these types of pictures with the subjects showing fuzzy edges at higher blow-up magnifications are harder to forge than higher quality sharp images in the sense that separate images stitched together can be easier to spot. I mean, it can be done, but the chances of having separate photos with the same poor resolution, bad lighting, color balance and so on is very low, and I've seldom seen convincing examples.

3. In this uncropped version I can see a finger – it must be Epstein's finger visible on the right... I think the angle shows its taker was approximately the same height as Andrew who is 5 feet 11 inches or 180 cm tall. Yes, it must have been Epstein, as he was 183 cm or 6 feet in height... and the expression on everyone's face shows they are very familiar with the taker. Also, I doubt whether either Maxwell, Epstein or Andrew would have let an inferior like a housekeeper take their image as a keepsake.

4. Ghislaine Maxwell is smiling and is in a relaxed stance leaning on a doorway, almost out of frame. But she seems smug and

happy to be witnessing the picture being taken. Hmm.... why is she looking so pleased with herself?

5. It's been taken upstairs on a landing, and the close proximity of Virginia and Andrew shows intimacy. You can see they definitely know each other, but he is not as relaxed about being photographed as she is.

6. Coming back to Maxwell, and why she looks a little too smug and self-satisfied... could this be the culmination of the weekend for her and Epstein? After all, they took Miss Giuffre all way to London for this. Did they tell Virginia to ask for a photo with Andrew? Maxwell has a kind of 'mission accomplished' look on her face...

7. Prince Andrew is hunched over a little, definitely not at ease with things. He's wearing a loose-fitting, fairly baggy shirt and trousers with no tie, though I understand he usually wears a suit and tie even in his leisure time in London. This is as close as he comes to 'letting his hair down', I think.

7. Virginia Giuffre's cheeks are a little red as if she's blushing, even when I adjust the contrast to high or low resolution. Why? Is she embarrassed by something, or a little nervous about being the focus of attention amongst the three adults?

8. Prince Andrew's right hand is in a claw gesture covering his groin. His hand hangs there limply in a kind of defensive stance, which Freudians might think rather significant...

9. I think the top of stairs position is very significant too, near the bedrooms. Why would a snap be taken there? If this picture was taken to compromise the prince, but without raising his suspicions too much, this would be a good place.

10. There is slight redness on either hip of Miss Giuffre below her crop-top and also on her left shoulder where she may have been held or squeezed firmly. Again, when I played with the contrast over and over, the darker colour is always there, despite the harsh glare of the flash coming both from the camera and its refection on the window pane behind.

11. The choice of clothes she's wearing, which are a low-fronted crop-top and skin-tight trousers, would be an innocent enough combination for a young kid, but not in this context. I mean, she looks so young, fresh-faced and vulnerable, and in my opinion she comes across as much younger than 17 years old, as she said she was at the time. I think she's been dressed up like 'Lolita' to emphasize her youth, which is a horrible thing to realize, given the circumstances of the picture.

12. 'You know what, I've read everything I can about this case, and after some consideration I'm highly suspicious this is a craftily-set honey trap arranged by either Epstein or Miss Giuffre herself or both. I'm pretty sure Virginia herself wasn't thinking of suing any of those adults twenty years later. It has the hallmarks of a 'trophy' picture, not for Andrew, but for Epstein himself... That would fit in with everything we know about Epstein. I think he calculated almost every move he made, and this is the photograph that proved Andrew and Miss Giuffre were together in Belgravia. There was no CCTV as he is said to have had in every room in his own houses, so yes, this could be the culmination of his wicked scheme to have Andrew compromised

and in his pocket. That's my take on the whole thing. Also, this photograph tells me that Andrew is at best naïve, but at worst very, very stupid to have a picture taken with his victim outside the bedrooms like that.

'By the way, I've analysed the picture using several different kinds of software for evidence of it being doctored or a composite of separate images put together. In my opinion it's definitely not a faked image, the lighting, perspective and resolution of all parts of that photograph are identical – and that includes the hand placed on that poor girl's waist.'

Now, thanks to the internet, the infamous image will endure and remain lodged in the communal memory. Once released, there is no way of erasing its horrible suggestion of sexual exploitation. Furthermore, while Andrew and Giuffre remain caught and frozen forever in the flash of the camera, there is the ever-present and vaguely sinister presence of Ghislaine Maxwell at the edge of the photograph.

And it could be argued that Maxwell being accepted into royal circles is very revealing of what the Royal Family behaves without the glare of publicity or public criticism – for our friend Ghislaine once had the freedom to enter Buckingham Palace at leisure. True, she was there to see Prince Andrew, and probably not other members of the household, but given the astonishing revelations about her that emerged at her trial in the USA – and the insights into her horrific inner nature – it is shocking that Maxwell was welcomed into royal circles for so long. Therefore, her role in lowering the reputation of the Royal Family deserves a closer look.

CHAPTER FIVE:
GHISLAINE MAXWELL – B.A. OXFORD (DECEPTION AND DEPRAVITY) DOUBLE FIRST – WITHOUT HONS

The question arises, how close was Ghislaine Maxwell to the royal family? She once walked freely in and out of Buckingham Palace almost as if she were herself royalty. Certainly, she was accepted through her friendship with Prince Andrew, sufficient for her to attend numerous events including a royal shooting weekend, and a party for the Duke of York's daughter.

The damning photograph of Prince Andrew with his arm around Virginia Giuffre – with a smiling Ghislaine Maxwell looking on – was taken at the time Maxwell was attending royal events. If, as has been suggested, Maxwell and Epstein set up the whole scene so as to ensnare the prince in scandal, it means the Royal Family was in effect infiltrated for blackmailing purposes.

One wonders that royal aids and security staff did not carry out due diligence checks and offer some timely advice about avoiding the sinister pair, instead of reacting only when the alleged wrong-doing led to a high profile court case.

And if that infamous photograph of Andrew and Giuffre really is telling a rather loathsome story of exploitation, complicity and entrapment, again, how was this allowed to happen when royal family members employ a number of advisors, aides and police security staff? Of course, the picture *could* have been nothing but an innocent keepsake taken so that the young Virginia Giuffre could tell her Mom she met a royal prince – but, given the cunning and devious natures of Jeffrey Epstein and Ghislaine Maxwell, is this really likely?

Because of this picture, and other damning information and evidence, Prince Andrew found himself in 'rather a pickle', as the English might say. But it is a pickle of his own making. After all, he chose his own friends and kept up his acquaintance with them for years after their criminality became widely known to the press and public. And without his liaisons with Epstein and Maxwell, it is hard to see how Andrew would have got himself into his current state of shame and total degradation. And there may be worse to come for him, should the continuing investigations into Maxwell and Epstein's affairs throw up new evidence in the future.

Andrew's extravagant lifestyle, while irksome to the British taxpayers, is not a crime. Nor is a love of beautiful women above the legal age of consent. But the accusations against Andrew that, as outlined earlier, that he had sexual encounters with Virginia Giuffre three times, including ones in the United States' Virgin Islands are ones that will not be forgotten by the British public. Furthermore, Ms Giuffre being used as a 'sex slave' by Epstein (when aged only 17) is a nefarious and felonious act punishable in *all* countries.

Virginia Giuffre, exploited for sex from the age of 15, was completely under the power of Epstein and Maxwell, and was allegedly paid £15,000 to endure the prince's sexual attentions. Ms Giuffre is adamant that Ghislaine Maxwell was instrumental in recruiting her, and dozens of other underage girls for sexual exploitation by Epstein and his friends.

Testimony in court indicated that Maxwell used extreme guile and subterfuge in recruiting young girls off the street.

According to several victims' accounts in court, she took part in many of the sexual encounters herself, as well as engaging in the 'training' of young girls in all manner of sexual practices to horribly entertain and please her boss.

It beggars belief that anyone would so demean themselves and risk their own criminal prosecution by enticing underage children into Epstein's clutches with various promises of money, friendship and protection, help with their future careers or other solicitations. But that is what came up in the evidence during Maxwell's trial in 2021. It revealed how girls as young as 13 were lured into the evil web spun by Maxwell and Epstein. Great pains, the witnesses and prosecution alleged, were taken to keep Epstein supplied with victims; indeed several accounts suggest Epstein thought he 'needed' three sexual encounters per day to satisfy his libido.

Maxwell, it was said, faithfully went out time and time again to procure the unfortunate girls. She is said to have cruised trailer parks, city streets and holiday resorts in search of her underage victims. Having been Epstein's girlfriend herself in the 1990's, and now maintaining a non-exclusive (to put it mildly) sexual relationship with him, it was said that Maxwell would stop at nothing to do his bidding. That he had some kind of psychological bond, an exploitative domination over her seems obvious enough. On the other hand, she did what she did willingly, diligently and, if the many witnesses in various court cases are to be believed, with great alacrity and obvious enjoyment.

Some have claimed this fawning relationship was really brought about simply by a love of money and the trappings of a 'high society' lifestyle – for Maxwell was well-paid and provided for by her 'boss' who seems even to have bought her town houses and all manner of luxuries. Whatever the truth may be, whether a twisted species of love, or misguided loyalty, or even as some suggested, the need for a wealthy 'sugar daddy' to replace her deceased, sometime rich and overbearing father is open to debate. One thing is clear: Epstein had a hold over her, and he used his position of power to get exactly what he wanted.

Other than exploiting underage girls, Epstein also sought to ingratiate himself with famous, wealthy and powerful people. He used the gregarious and well-connected Maxwell to facilitate and organise his often devious schemes. And it is through Maxwell that Prince Andrew came to be drawn much closer to Jeffrey Epstein, leading ultimately to his ruination and public shaming in 2022.

Maxwell began spending more time with Andrew in the late 1990's, when the two were frequently seen together. There were newspaper stories and pictures linking the pair with trips to racecourses, parties, nightclubs, weddings and various society gatherings. They were photographed together eight times in the year 2000 alone. On many of these outings Maxwell was accompanied by Epstein; but on many occasions it was just she and Andrew who were seen together. It has been questioned whether this liaison was more than just a platonic friendship, for, as stated earlier, Epstein and Maxwell were certainly not noted for sexual fidelity to one another. Could it have been that Maxwell was required by Epstein to reel Andrew in, then get him into the billionaire's social circle? Certainly Epstein described himself as 'a collector of famous people'. What is not in dispute is that Epstein wanted Andrew as a 'friend', or at least as a close, useful contact; and it was Maxwell who could get her lover-employer what he wanted.

This was easy enough to do, since Ghislaine Maxwell and Andrew had been friends since she'd attended Oxford University in the early 1980's. They met through mutual society acquaintances. Both of them being well-known 'socialites', they ran into each other frequently before becoming closer. When together they seemed to have something of a rapport, one of their mutual acquaintances reported, though she always seemed rather too 'pushy'. [6]

What is not in dispute is that, from the mid 1990's their friendship really took off. At her invitation Andrew, once described by friends as a 'couch potato', began attending many more social events in Britain and around the world. Having divorced his wife in May 1996, Andrew was now more at liberty to take up his old pursuits of 'partying' and seeking the company of beautiful women. Friends of Andrew have strongly suggested that Ghislaine Maxwell was instrumental in rejuvenating Andrew's social life at this time, which soon involved travelling to Jeffrey Epstein's houses in New York, the US Virgin Islands and New Mexico. In return, the prince invited Maxwell and Epstein to royal residences including Windsor, Balmoral and Sandringham.

It is not clear to what extent Andrew himself was lured or cunningly drawn into Maxwell's and Epstein's devious world of overblown socialite swagger, or if he in fact leapt into it voluntarily with both eyes open. From what is known of Epstein and Maxwell, Andrew would have been no match for their scheming and guile. But what is true is that he spent a deal of time at their residences, travelled with them around the world, and willingly accepted their company and hospitality.

It goes without saying that he was in no way put off by Ghislaine Maxwell's dubious background. She was the daughter of disgraced news tycoon and shady businessman Robert Maxwell, who was found dead after swindling around half a billion pounds of his employees' pension money. Many have insisted Maxwell senior was very closely tied with the Israeli secret service, for which he is said to have spied. The same accusation has been levelled at Ghislaine herself. On a more mundane level, she was said by others in the 'smart set' to be a social climber who insinuated herself amongst the rich and famous first in the United Kingdom, then in the United States where she re-located in 1991 to make a fresh start.

There, in Manhattan, New York, She lamented to an acquaintance that she was now 'broke', having 'only' $80,000 annually to her name (a trust fund set up by her late father).[7] On her left pinkie finger she wore a signet ring, an affectation she adopted to emulate the aristocratic set in England whose rings worn there often bear a family crest. Thus, fellow upper-crust socialites might recognize each other amongst the riff-raff of 'nouveau riche' individuals, or, heaven forbid, the commoners and 'poor folk' who are to be avoided at all costs. By all accounts Maxwell practised an extreme form of this discriminatory behaviour, which partially explains her utter lack of sympathy and empathy for her later victims. British snobbery, as practised by many – but not all – of the upper classes has not died out as some suggest, but fossilized into a more modern code of practice.

Ghislaine Maxwell's version was to treat with disdain and contempt anyone not worthy of her most noble attention. This

43

was achieved by several stylized methods. Ignoring the 'lower orders', by turning one's back on them if not in the mood to answer a question is a behavioural 'norm' for the elite, as is averting one's gaze in annoyance, or giving a short, sharp reprimand to silence somebody speaking out of turn. To avoid having to do this too often at Epstein's houses, she had a laminated sheet of 'rules' that servants and those under her power had to observe. These regulations included:

1. *No eye contact with your employer or his guests.*
2. *Stand aside when passing in a corridor.*
3. *Speak only when spoken to.*
4. *Be showered, deodorised and well groomed so as not to offend your employers.*
5. *Stand to attention when receiving orders.*
6. *Do whatever you are told to do without protest.*
7. *Never divulge to anybody whatsoever what you see or hear in your employer's household.*
8. *No contact by phone or pictures to be sent to the outside world while working.*
9. *Anticipate what your superiors want and carry out your duties without fuss, undue haste or nuisance.*
10. *Never use a lavatory, wash basin, towel, utensil or any item whatsoever reserved for your employer. Use only your own facilities at all times.*
11. *You will sign a non-disclosure contract.*
12. *You will do nothing to bring into discredit your employer or any member of his household, or any of his guests.*

These rules are reputedly her version of the ones taught and enacted in British aristocratic households, and might be entirely familiar to Prince Andrew.

In his BBC 'Newsnight' interview with the journalist Emily Maitlis, Andrew himself, said:

"I live in an institution at Buckingham Palace which has members of staff walking around all the time and I don't wish to appear grand but there were a lot of people who were walking around Jeffrey Epstein's house. As far as I was aware, they were staff... I didn't, if you see what I mean, interact with them in a way that was, you know, what are you doing here, why are you here, what's going on?"

In other words mere servants are hardly noticed or engaged with, except when something is required of them. 'Social control' is the name of the game when there is a large household to run. Treatment of servants in an offhand and dictatorial manner is one of many things Maxwell, Epstein and Prince Andrew are said to have had in common that helped bond them together.

Would Prince Andrew have objected to Epstein and Maxwell's shared love of conspicuous, over-consumption of every luxury money can buy? Or the burning of enormous quantities of aviation fuel for the billionaire's private jet and helicopters flown on trivial pleasure trips around the world? The heartless treatment of those they perceived as their social inferiors as beings beneath their dignity and therefore unworthy of their sympathy? That is for *you* to decide.

Indeed, is it possible at all to be fabulously wealthy and powerful at all without a corresponding lack of *sympathy*, the instinctive feeling of sorrow and regret at another's discomfort, or without a deficiency in *empathy* the ability to imagine oneself in another's plight that leads us to *help* others, rather than *exploit* them?

And how did Ghislaine Maxwell and Jeffrey Epstein treat those less wealthy and privileged than themselves? Ghislaine Maxwell's fellow socialite Christina Oxenberg[7] recounts how Maxwell talked about the children she picked up off the streets, or lifted from the Palm Beach area trailer parks. After explaining that Epstein claimed to need three sexual encounters with young girls per day to satisfy the paedophile's 'biological needs' Maxwell declared:

'The girls. They are nothing! They are trash!' [8]

There is a great gap between being a friend and associate of Maxwell and Epstein, and actually joining in their depraved acts against children. And yet Virginia Giuffre insists Prince Andrew had sex with her on three separate occasions when she was seventeen. One encounter was, allegedly, in Maxwell's flat in London, which gave rise to the infamous picture on the landing; another was in Epstein's Manhattan townhouse; the third on the Little St. James residence in the U.S. Virgin Islands.

Epstein and Maxwell believed they were above the law. Is this a 'royal' trait too? And what about the use of hugely expensive legal teams to shield and deflect the accusations of the victims of Epstein's depravity? Epstein's huge band of lawyers, faced with impossible odds, got him a sweetheart deal of 13 months jail in 2005 when he should have got life. Maxwell's own lawyers attempted to get her off the hook by all manner of strategies, and even after the trial moved to get her released through an appeal based on the allegation that a member of her original jury was a victim of abuse and so ineligible to serve at her trial in 2021.

And how would Prince Andrew have fared, when thrown

into the amphitheatre of a court of civil law? A famous lawyer once said: 'It is a simple enough task to assert one's innocence when the conscience is clear – but not so simple to cover up one's guilt with a tissue of lies when the prosecution's lawyers are highly competent at their job.'[9] One thing is clear: the scandal of a trial airing charges of a heinous sexual nature was certainly going to do Andrew no favours, and was unlikely to restore his reputation, *even if he had won*.

CHAPTER SIX:
WHEN RANDY ANDY MET DEGENERATE JEFF

If being friends with Ghislaine Maxwell proved to be a liability for Prince Andrew, being a pal of Jeffrey Epstein was an even greater calamity. Prince Andrew told the TV presenter Emily Maitlis he first met Epstein, a wealthy hedge fund manager, in 1999. However, Andrew is being a little economical with the truth here. In fact, the prince encountered him long, long before this.

Ghislaine Maxwell was dating Epstein from the mid 1990's, and there has been speculation as to whether Andrew met the billionaire through her. But a letter written to The (British) Times newspaper in March 2011 solves this dispute. Retired Major Alastair Watson was the Duke's private secretary in the early 1990's, and he confirms Andrew *did* meet Epstein many years earlier. In the correspondence Watson, while denying the duke was good friends with Saif Gaddafi, the son of the late monster-tyrant Colonel Gaddafi of Libya, he did state that *'There has been widespread comment on the duke's relationship with Jeffrey Epstein. The duke has known Mr Epstein since being introduced to him in the early 1990s.'*

Andrew's memory is very poor, it would seem. For the record, Watson concludes his letter with the rather stuffy rebuttal of the accusations of Virginia Giuffre and the world press thus:

'The insinuations and innuendos that have been made in relation to the duke are without foundation.'

But those are rather more than 'insinuations and innuendos', Major! A civil trial loomed over him, with witnesses from both sides of the Atlantic prepared to testify on behalf of Virginia Giuffre.

Returning to the subject of Epstein, 1999 was in fact the first year in which the prince and the businessman were linked in *press reports* in the UK and US. But is it possible the foundations of a seemingly close friendship were laid almost a decade earlier?

Though Andrew first flew with Epstein on his private Gulfstream jet into the US Virgin Islands in February of 1999, curiously, The Daily Mail reported that Andrew's ex-wife Sarah Ferguson had appeared in the logbook a full 10 months earlier (also travelling to Epstein's Virgin Island retreat). Though the royal couple had divorced in 1996, they had, and still do maintain, a very close relationship. It seems odd that Sarah Ferguson should have been on close enough terms with Epstein to fly on his jet before Prince Andrew. This is no less mysterious, when one considers that Andrew claims to have first encountered Epstein only as Ghislaine Maxwell's boyfriend. What is clear, however, is that both Andrew and his ex-wife were on sufficiently good terms with the billionaire paedophile to enjoy his lavish hospitality.

One good turn deserves another. In June 2000 Epstein and Maxwell were invited by Andrew to a party at Windsor Castle hosted by none other than the late Queen. This event, dubbed 'Dance of the Decades' was attended by more than 500 guests. It celebrated four royal birthdays, including Prince Andrew's 40th.

Prince Andrew downplayed Epstein's presence in his BBC interview, saying that Epstein was only there as Ghislaine Maxwell's 'plus one' and emphasized that the couple from New

York were there as his personal guests, thus exonerating the Queen from any blame.

It has been observed that at this time Andrew seemed particularly close to Maxwell, being seen accompanying her to private parties and celebrity functions both in the UK and around the world. Could it be that the Prince and Maxwell were more than good friends? Certainly one of Andrew's bodyguards thought so,[10] observing how Maxwell came and went from Prince Andrew's private apartments at Buckingham Palace so many times that the staff suspected an intimate relationship was taking place. Whatever the truth, as stated earlier, it is well known that neither Maxwell nor Epstein were in any way bothered by their partner having physical relationships with whomsoever they wished.

Andrew and Maxwell were present together at the wedding of the prince's old flame Aurelia Cecil in Wiltshire, England, in September 2000, and also at a Halloween party held by model Heidi Klum in Manhattan a month later. At the latter, Maxwell was reportedly dressed rather resplendently in gold lame and a blonde wig at the 'Hookers and Pimps' themed celebration. Andrew donned clothes only a little more casual than usual, perhaps thinking this qualified him as looking suitably 'common'.

Next, in December 2000, Epstein and Maxwell were photographed at Sandringham attending a pheasant shoot. Andrew called this (in his infamous TV interview) a 'straightforward shooting weekend', though staff at the country house had reportedly been advised of guests arriving at short notice for a surprise birthday party. Prince Andrew and Maxwell were also seen in 2001 on a several holidays together including one to Florida and another to Thailand, as reported by the UK's Evening Standard. The paper also said that Epstein had joined them on no less than five such occasions over the previous year.

Andrew stated to the BBC that he saw Epstein 'a maximum of three times a year'. He owned up to using Epstein's private plane to visit Little St James, the billionaire's home in the United States Virgin Islands, and said he had visited Epstein at his Palm Beach, Florida and New York residences. On Andrew's own admission, these visits continued even after Epstein was indicted for child-sex offences in 2005, and amazingly, Andrew even attended Epstein's Manhattan mansion after the billionaire had been charged, imprisoned, and released on parole in 2009.

Given the seriousness of the charges against Jeffrey Epstein and the fact that allegations against the paedophile-billionaire had begun in 2005 when the parents of a 14-year-old girl first told police in Florida that Epstein had assaulted their daughter at his Palm Beach residence, it is to be wondered at that Andrew continued his extremely close ties with Epstein. Did he know of all these allegations? More importantly, did he care?

Unbelievably, in July 2006 Epstein and Maxwell attended a masked ball held at Windsor Castle to celebrate Andrew's elder daughter Beatrice's 18th birthday. The theme of the evening was 1888, and 550 guests donned period costumes.

Only the previous month, Epstein had been charged with one count of solicitation of prostitution. Prince Andrew said Epstein had been invited as a guest of Ghislaine Maxwell, and that he was unaware of 'what was going on in the United States.'

The British press questioned whether this was plausible, given his closeness with Epstein, and especially with Maxwell, and the magnitude of the accusations. Furthermore, given Epstein's predilection for young girls, who were everywhere to be seen in his households (and with awful images of naked and semi-naked children on walls all over his residences) it is hard to fathom why Andrew would want Epstein at his young daughter's birthday party at all, especially with his other daughter, Princess Eugenie (aged 16 at the time) being present too.

When Epstein was formally accused in 2006 of grooming and coercing girls as young as 14 to perform sex acts at his Manhattan and Florida homes between 2002 and 2005, still this was not considered sufficiently serious for Andrew to keep away from his friend.

Certainly, the evidence suggests Prince Andrew was far closer to Epstein than he cares to admit. Even after Epstein's controversial 'sweetheart' leniency legal deal in 2008 saw him plead guilty to a lesser charge of soliciting a minor for prostitution, and spend thirteen months of incarceration, Andrew was nothing cowed by Epstein's criminal convictions and disgrace. Not only did he continue contact with Epstein, he was prepared even to visit him in New York upon his release.

Epstein himself, though due to serve eighteen months' prison in a county minimum security stockade, was controversially freed five months early. He had been allowed to roam freely in a part of the jail, and was soon put into the county's work-release program. During that time, he was taken to his office, spending six days a week and eighteen hours a day there. Two women, one of whom was only 17, said they were trafficked to Epstein's office to allegedly have paid sex with him there. It would appear that Epstein's money and power allowed him to carry on his illicit behaviour even while being punished.[11]

In December 2010, shortly after the tycoon had served his sentence, the duke was photographed with Epstein in New York's Central Park. Prince Andrew maintained in his BBC Newsnight interview that he had travelled across the Atlantic to end his friendship with Epstein and was having that difficult conversation with him when they were photographed in the Park. Prince Andrew admitted he attended a small dinner Party while he was there, but denied it was to celebrate Epstein's release.

At this party were, reportedly, Woody Allen , the subject of sexual misconduct investigations in the 1990's, his wife Soon-Yi Previn, and Charlie Rose, the CBS anchorman who was later fired from his post after a spate of allegations that he was a sexual predator. One of those at the party said that Prince Andrew had been the guest of honour. Footage released by the British Mail on Sunday newspaper showed Prince Andrew inside the paedophile's Manhattan mansion around the same time. One reporter commented that he looked relaxed and comfortable in casual attire at the door, waving farewell to a female woman guest.

The prince told the BBC that he 'let the side down' by visiting Epstein, and that he regretted staying there. As to the reports of many young girls coming and going from the townhouse at the time, he said: 'I never saw them.' Andrew added that Epstein's house had people coming in and out all the time 'like a railway station'.

If these comments were designed to downplay Prince Andrew's relationship with the convicted sex offender it backfired badly. These words, and the rest of the interview for that matter, resulted in a storm of criticism in the United Kingdom and across the world.

Even at the time, newspaper reports in 2011 on the Andrew-Epstein friendship were scathing of his connection to a convicted paedophile. Later that year, Prince Andrew received more bad publicity when his ex-wife Sarah Ferguson was proven to have accepted £15,000 from Epstein, reportedly to pay off some of her considerable debts.

The harsh public reaction to all this forced Andrew to resign his role as a UK trade envoy in July 2011. At this time, Prince Andrew rather belatedly called his friendship with Epstein 'a mistake'.

It took until July 2019 for Epstein to be finally charged in New York with further allegations of sex trafficking and other felonies relating to his predatory nature, and he was due to face trial the following year (facing up to 45 years in prison if convicted).

As it turned out, 2019 was a fateful year for Prince Andrew. Early in the year, legal documents revealed that Johanna Sjoberg, another alleged Epstein victim, claimed Andrew touched her breast while sitting on a couch inside Epstein's Manhattan house in 2001.

Buckingham Palace was quick to deny the allegations, calling them 'categorically untrue'. But the British media now had its ears pricked when on August 9th Virginia Giuffre's lawyers succeeded in their bid to have 2,000 pages of legal documents unsealed concerning the abuse of young girls by

Epstein and Maxwell. Prince Andrew was among those named for allegedly having had sex with the trafficked Giuffre three times in three separate locations. Despite denials by Andrew's Buckingham Palace advisors and legal team, speculation has been rife ever since. It took until January 2022 for Giuffre's team to get the go-ahead for a civil case for August 2022.

By this time Geoffrey Berman, the U.S. attorney for the Southern District of New York, had been removed by then President Donald Trump on 20 June 2020. Unproven allegations suggested that Trump may have removed Berman partly because of the embarrassment heaped on Prince Andrew by the attorney pressing him for information.

But, even with Berman removed, Virginia Giuffre's lawyers led by David Boise were still able to press ahead with their case. Judge Lewis Kaplan finally ruled in September 2021 that papers had been legally served on Prince Andrew, and by the end of November 2021 he made it plain that a trial would be scheduled for October to December 2022.

Finally Prince Andrew was compelled to address his accusers head on – either by opposing Virginia Giuffre in a civil trial in New York, or by somehow getting her to agree on a settlement that would involve paying her, or her charities, an eye-watering sum of money.

There was also the small matter of the wording of that settlement, which would of course try to portray the prince in the least damaging way possible. But before the settlement was decided upon, there was still a deal of ugly manoeuvres between the two parties, as the English legal team made plain what deplorable tactics they were prepared to employ to forcefully state their case.

CHAPTER SEVEN: 'VICTIM BLAMING AND GASLIGHTING' IT JUST GETS WORSE AND WORSE...

On 16th January 2022 Prince Andrew's legal team decided the best way of defending him against Virginia Giuffre's accusations was by demanding copies of her mental health records, including confidential notes from psychological counselling sessions. Records of prescriptions, and details of her 'alleged emotional and psychological harm and damages' should also be surrendered. Furthermore, Andrew's lawyers proposed questioning Giuffre's psychologist, Dr Judith Lightfoot about the plaintiff's mental health.

It was also suggested that Andrew's team might employ a psychologist to utilize the 'theory of false memories' to cast doubt on Ms Giuffre's memory, and so discredit whatever information came to light in her pre-trial depositions, or later in court.

This strategy is exactly what Ghislaine Maxwell's lawyers had tried to use in 2021 – without any successful outcome, it must be said. Considering that the Royal Family is (usually) ultra-sensitive to public opinion, this news of how the Prince's legal experts proposed to defend him was astonishing. Rather predictably, it caused a huge storm of criticism, both on social media and in the Press.

Virginia Giuffre had an awful lot of public support in Britain; which is more than can be said for Andrew. Ms Giuffre's lawyer, David Boies, told the British popular newspaper 'The Daily Mail' on 18th January 2022 that when Maxwell's team tried the same tactic:

'It didn't end well. People may misremember a lot of things,

but they don't misremember sexual abuse by a prince of England'.

The damage and controversy created by this kind of public relations nightmare is immense, and irreversible. On the same day as Boise spoke to the Daily Mail, the online edition of the Independent (18th January 2022) had its finger on the pulse of public opinion when it carried an interview of Dr Charlotte Proudman, a prominent barrister who is known for her feminist and women's rights work in the academic and legal sphere. In response to the accusations against Prince Andrew's representatives of 'victim blaming' and 'gaslighting' (making a victim doubt their own sanity by psychological trickery) she stated that:

'Using the most intimate and personal mental health or medical records is victim blaming and victim shaming. Why does the accused have the right to intrude into their entire lives? Why is the court allowing this? This is an abusive process. This isn't a fair hearing, this is a very unfair hearing for victims of trauma. Many victims won't come forward to report rape or abuse because they fear that their counselling or medical records will be accessed by the accused. Everything they told a professional in a confidential setting is then poured over by the accused to find inconsistencies.'

Dr Proudman added that she believed Andrew's strategy was in her opinion 'highly abusive'. She said that it amounted to 'gaslighting' because by suggesting that a plaintiff's version of reality is false and that their memory is faulty causes a persons' whole sense of self' to be questioned.

She continued: 'We don't say to the accused that they have false memories and that's why they cannot remember sexually *assaulting the complainant. Perhaps we should.'*

Judge Lewis Kaplan denied the prince's team's move to have the sexual assault lawsuit against Andrew dismissed. He was, as stated earlier, now prepared to go to trial in mid-2022.

Virginia Giuffre consistently maintained that she was not only fighting for her own sake. She is a campaigner for justice for sex trafficking victims. In Britain, as in the rest of the world, she has garnered strong support from many organisations supporting women's and victims' rights.

One prominent lawyer supporting her cause is Harriet Wistrich, founding director of the Centre for Women's Justice. She was, like Dr Proudman, forthright in her criticism of Prince Andrew. She complained to the Independent that the behaviour of Andrew's lawyers showed the 'worst forms of victim-blaming in a sex offence case.' These, she said, *'move beyond the legitimate investigation of evidence that may cast doubt on the accuracy and credibility of the victim's allegations, to a wholesale attack on her character'.* She also said that the use of the false memory argument was a controversial and largely *'discredited approach'.*

Jayne Butler, chief executive of Rape Crisis England and Wales, weighed in to the argument by saying that counselling was an important part of a victim and survivor's ability to deal with the trauma they have faced, and that allowing access to personal counselling notes would be intrusive and possibly re-traumatising. Her organisation said that counselling and therapy notes should be protected from disclosure to give counsellors the same confidentiality as is found in the legal profession.

Andrea Simon, director of the End Violence Against Women

Coalition, said that survivors of sexual violence had the right to receive therapy without the threat of being discredited in court. Furthermore: *'Scrutinising therapy notes in a courtroom strips them of their context and sends a message loud and clear that it is survivors who are on trial, rather than the men who raped them.'*

Yet another blow occurred on the 19 Jan 2022. The Prince's lawyers would also need to address the future testimony of Shukri Walker, who alleged she visited Tramp nightclub in 2001 when she saw Prince Andrew with Virginia Giuffre, along with Ghislaine Maxwell. Ms Walker said she was willing provide evidence in the civil sexual assault trial.[12]

As a result of all this disastrous publicity, moves were afoot in Buckingham Palace to try to limit the damage, or at least appease the most vocal critics of Prince Andrew. A few days later, Andrew was stripped of many of his titles, and his social media accounts were removed. This included his official Twitter, Facebook and Instagram accounts. He was still listed on the Royal Family website, albeit with the prefix 'His Royal Highness' title deleted, along with his list of military and other honorary titles. It would appear that orders were issued from sources close to him that he should not be allowed to continue to have direct social media contact that might further inflame public sentiment against him, or be a conduit for public rage.

Shame, shame, and yet more shame. One is reminded of Edward VIII's vilification by some elements of the British press around the time of his forced abdication in 1937, of his being pushed out of the limelight after his exile, and his successor's refusal to allow his wife the title of 'Her Royal Highness'.

But Edward VIII had been guilty only of wanting to marry a divorced American lady; whereas, Andrew stood accused of far worse things. And he faced more stinging blows on 19 January 2022 when there were political moves to have his team of three security police officers removed. This service reportedly cost the British taxpayers $380,000 for salaries and other costs. But it was said the late Queen had stepped in to ensure her son continued to be protected.

However, a report in the Daily Mail on 19th January 2022 said Queen Elizabeth had refused to cover a real estate debt of Prince Andrew of $7.6 over costs of a luxury Swiss ski chalet. Presumably Andrew and family would now have to rely on the charity of friends when it comes to staying in Switzerland on skiing excursions, or heaven forbid, *pay* for their accommodation.

The point is, Prince Andrew is now seen as an embarrassment to the royal family. One wonders what further horrors lie in store for him now that the Queen has passed away, when it is very possible King Charles and his son Prince William will require some political and physical distancing from 'Prince Pariah', as the popular press had now dubbed him. This pejorative name anticipated even more adverse publicity when Giuffre's court action seemed imminent and its preceding depositions would put Andrew under even more scrutiny. But the handle has been used more than once on social media posts, and will no doubt turn up again and again.

Further bad news was also forthcoming. During Maxwell's trial, several of her acquaintances, who were referred to only by their numbers (or as *John Doe's*) asked the court that their identities remain secret. But Judge Kaplan gave notice that these might be named, even without a trial, and that information about them be revealed. With Maxwell's lawyers now consenting to the anonymous 'non-parties' being unmasked, there was speculation as to which famous names were among them.

On 19th January 2022 in a document known as 'the plaintiff's brief, John Does 17, 53, 54, 55, 56 73 93 and 151's were revealed to have made objections to the unsealing of their identities. But who exactly are these objectors? They were said to have had an 'opinion on why the information must not be revealed'.

During Maxwell's trial in 2021 these non parties were protected by her lawyers. But why was she shielding these non-parties, now shown to number 16 in all? Obviously if she was protecting them they weren't victims, but people she knew who might be unhappy – or in trouble – if their names were suddenly thrust into the limelight.

Judge Kaplan brought out a 'Preliminary Statement' which referred to 'annoyance' or 'embarrassment' which was not sufficient grounds to keep the document sealed. He said that losing anonymity would not be dangerous to the hidden parties, though 'potentially salacious information' might come to light.

Was Andrew's name amongst those 'John Does' being shielded from public view? There was much speculation on this. Perhaps, as Andrew's lawyers would have us believe, the prince is wholly innocent, and the victim of a 'smash-and-grab' attempt to force him to pay vast sums of money in compensation for something he didn't do. It is possible. However, it would appear the Royal Family are taking no chances, and moves have been made to make it plain that

Andrew, whether guilty or innocent, acted alone, and his behaviour is not condoned.

Something of the huge embarrassment felt by other members of the Royal Family was revealed on 19 January 2022 when Prince William, the Duke of Cambridge, was just leaving the Foundling Museum in London with his wife. When a member of a TV news crew asked: 'Do you support Prince Andrew?' a smiling William leaned closer to hear – and then, comprehending the question, his smile faded and he stiffened. Adopting a stony face, he walked swiftly on, saying – absolutely nothing.

As is well known, on 15 February 2022 Prince Andrew eventually agreed to pay a settlement to accuser Virginia Giuffre, and a US district judge agreed to dismiss her lawsuit against the Duke of York.

Giuffre's attorney David Boies said in a statement to the news media: "The payment was received, the settlement we announced last month has been completed. We are obviously very pleased with the outcome."

Boies would not disclose the amount the two parties agreed upon. The Prince was not available for comment, but his lawyers' submitted to court a document stating:

"Prince Andrew intends to make a substantial donation to Ms. Giuffre's charity in support of victims' rights.

"Prince Andrew has never intended to malign Ms Giuffre's character, and he accepts that she has suffered both as an established victim of abuse and as a result of unfair public attacks.

"It is known that Jeffrey Epstein trafficked countless young girls over many years. Prince Andrew regrets his association with

Epstein, and commends the bravery of Ms Giuffre and other survivors in standing up for themselves and others.

"He pledges to demonstrate his regret for his association with Epstein by supporting the fight against the evils of sex trafficking, and by supporting its victims."

A second document, a letter addressed to US judge Lewis A Kaplan, who has been overseeing the case, said: *"We write jointly with counsel for defendant to advise the court that the parties reached a settlement in principle of the above-referenced action."*

Thus ended the legal threat of a court hearing that might have seen Prince Andrew grilled over the fine details of his associations with Epstein and Maxwell, and which would have sought to prove beyond doubt that Virginia Giuffre's accusations were true.

The settlement was very much a case of 'damage limitation' on the part of Andrew and the Royal Family. While no admission of guilt was stated or implied, the world in general must draw its own conclusions as to why such a substantial sum of money (estimated by the press to be $12,000,000) might have been paid.

Clearly, Virginia Giuffre and David Boies considered the outcome of the legal action as a victory.

No doubt to Andrew it represented a great relief from stress and possible further trouble.

But to the rest of the Royal Family the whole sorry affair was nothing more than an unmitigated public relations disaster which will besmirch their reputation and standing with the British and world public for a very long time indeed.

CHAPTER EIGHT:
SNUBS, SNOBS, AND SOCIAL MEDIA REVELATIONS

When the usually affable Prince William blanked the press by turning his back on them and refusing to answer their questions, he was demonstrating a classic behavioural trait of the British aristocracy. This type of snub was also used by the future king Charles on a reporter while visiting a forest in Scotland on 14th January 2022 (and recorded by BBC TV news). A polite enquiry as to what Charles thought about his brother Andrew being embroiled in a scandal caused Charles to pause momentarily. Then, as a royal aid interposed himself between his boss and the journalist, Prince Charles adopted a stony face, turned his back on the reporter and strode on.

Were these just isolated instances of royal ill-temper, petulance or temporary lack of grace? Certainly not – servants, courtiers, gamekeepers and others employed in royal households have reported receiving the same snub if speaking out of turn. Indeed, the silent snub (a deadly insult if directed at an 'equal') seems to be the standard rebuke for breaking royal protocol. Perhaps, in an age where slinging treasonous – or insolent – subjects into the Tower of London is no longer allowed, the royal snub must suffice as the ultimate weapon of royal reprimand.

And, when it comes to treating commoners with disdain, Prince Andrew is said to be way ahead of his peers. Newspapers again had him on their front pages on January after a former maid revealed how Andrew had mistreated her at Buckingham Palace in the 1990's. Charlotte Briggs, formerly a palace administrator, was given the job of maid in Prince Andrew's part of the building. He'd recently moved back in following his divorce from Sarah Ferguson. Nobody else had wanted the job – the prince had a reputation for being foul-tempered and difficult to please. Before long, she was being reduced to tears and felt 'miserable' in the role. She said that even leaving a tiny gap between the huge floor-to-ceiling curtains caused outbursts of swearing from Prince Andrew. When Andrew's terrier bit her, he laughed. She was also rebuked sharply *for putting the prince's collection of teddy bears in the wrong order* after cleaning the room. A laminated sheet (like those used by Maxwell) had the teddy bear positions in a diagram that had to be followed down to the last detail.

A royal gamekeeper, who does not want to be identified for fear of losing his job, gave the following insight:

'Commoners are not considered proper people; we're useful, quaint and funny but regarded as being about same level of importance as the donkey that pulls the cart. You get a certain respect for being good at your job, but as I was told by the keepers who'd been here longer, making a small mistake or speaking out of turn can mean getting the cold shoulder treatment, or worse, being told you don't 'fit in' – which means you get asked to find another job. Basically, when it comes to gamekeeping, nothing has changed at all since Queen Victoria's day. If anything, the snobbery is actually worse now than it ever was.' [13]

A royal protection officer policeman, on duty at a pheasant shoot in Helmingham Suffolk attended by the Queen, the Duke of Edinburgh, Prince Charles (as he then was) and Prince Andrew spoke off the record to one of the shoot's 'picking-up' team (dog handlers employed to find the shot game birds) who later conveyed this information about 'the royals' to the author:

'This job's usually straightforward enough, and if you don't mind travelling it's better than sitting in an office all day. But some of them can be a bit sharp tongued, like Princess Anne when she gets in a strop. Mostly, they're easy to get along with, like the Queen and Charles, but Andrew is by far the worst one to deal with, and some days he can be a right pain in the a*s.' [14]

Now, these bits of gossip have until now escaped public scrutiny, but what they do show are glimpses of the 'them' and 'us' mentality of the Royal Family. If their attitude, their core belief, is that they are not simply richer, but actually superior, that their lives matter so much more than non-royal 'subjects', this would have serious implications for the way the public perceive them. It would also imply that the friendly handshaking and polite smiles at public events are not genuine at all. Aristocrats and royals have been heard to describe those they perceive as commoners as 'non-U' people, representing the phrase 'non-us', or 'not our sort of people.'

This would explain why servants are sometimes treated with scorn. A former police bodyguard recalled the story of how he observed an inexperienced valet of Prince Charles' (as his majesty was then called) come unstuck. On his first morning in his new job the valet got most things correct, including putting the right amount of toothpaste on the royal toothbrush, waking the prince at the right time and even bringing him his morning tea nice and hot. But then he stuck his foot in it and asked 'And what would you like to wear this morning, sir?' and was hit with a torrent of anger, as the usually mild-mannered Charles retorted:

'How should I bloody-well know? I pay you to decide what I

wear! Look in the diary, man!'[15]

Royal Family members are not the only employers who treat their servants with scorn and condescension, rather like an unfortunate house cat that gets kicked by a cruel householder when a bad mood takes him. However, living on taxpayer's money as they do, and courting public approval and reverence, some might see an overriding hypocrisy in the way some members of the Royal Family present themselves in public, and how they conduct themselves in private. The image being projected seems like an attempt to promote benevolent leadership – whereas the anecdotal evidence is of some members of The Firm, as they call themselves, behaving like bullying bosses out of touch with twenty-first century values.

On the subject of out-of-touch royal values, the people of Britain – and world - were shocked by the allegation of Meghan Markle and Prince Harry that a senior member of the Royal Family had *'concerns and conversations about how dark his skin might be when he's born'.* This bombshell statement occurred as Meghan Markle was being interviewed by Oprah Winfrey in March of 2021. Meghan said there had been 'several conversations' initiated by one of Harry's relatives about Archie's skin tone, and 'what that would mean or look like'. Oprah Winfrey then asked if there would be concerns from some quarters that her child would be 'too brown', to which Meghan replied: *'If that is the assumption you are making, that is a pretty safe one.'*

When Prince Harry married Meghan Markle and so brought her, for a time, into the Royal Family, she was able to see the goings-on at Buckingham Palace and in court circles with the fresh perspective of a young, non-aristocratic female American

– and she was amazed and confused by the strange world she now found herself in. She was expected to show deference to more senior royal family members, engage in endless visits and engagements, and be under the spotlight of public and press scrutiny for large portions of every day. The pace was relentless, the pressures punishing, even for a woman accustomed to a certain level of fame and media gossip back home in America.

In her interview with Oprah Winfrey she describes being driven almost to suicide by the pressure of royal life, of how staff could not, or would not, help her when she told them her mental health was suffering. Indeed, she claims that elements in Buckingham Palace were putting out information to the news outlets that cast her in a bad light. She says she felt that she had to speak out because:

'I don't know how they could expect that after all of this time, we would still just be silent if there is an active role that The Firm is playing in perpetuating falsehoods about us.'

She further alleges that the royal staff assigned to assist her in fact ended up accusing her of upsetting the Duchess of Cambridge, and even bullying members of Palace staff – though she says *she* was the one being pushed beyond her ability to cope. She felt isolated, trapped, she said, because:

'You couldn't just go. You couldn't. I mean, you have to understand, as well, when I joined that family, that was the last time, until we came here, that I saw my passport, my driver's licence, my keys. All that gets turned over. I didn't see any of that any more.'

Things grew so bad, that when she and Harry attended a public event in the Albert Hall she was thinking suicidal thoughts, while all the time having to put on a brave face and pretend to the public that she was not in mental turmoil.

Eventually, in 2021 Meghan Markle and Prince Harry left Britain for the USA. Part of the reason, she says, is that her children would receive no protection in the U.K. from its security forces. The hostility of the British press also played a role, she says; and Harry explained that they had to make the decision to leave 'for my own mental health, my wife's and for Archie's as well. Because I could see where this was headed.'

He is alluding to his own mother's issues with mental health, negative portrayals in the tabloid press, and conflicts within the complex decision-making administrative staff at the palace. In particular, Harry expresses disappointment and hurt that neither 'senior Palace staff' as he calls them, nor 'members of my family' seemed able to help combat the tabloid press 'in their colonial [racist] undertones of articles and headlines written about Meghan.'

His explanation is very telling:

'I... am acutely aware of where my family stand and how scared they are of the tabloids turning on them.'

Here Oprah Winfrey, for the umpteenth time is surprised, and says: 'Turning on them for what? They're the Royal Family!'

Harry's explanation hits the nail squarely on the head:

'There is this invisible . . . what's termed or referred to as the 'invisible contract' behind closed doors between the institution and the tabloids, the UK tabloids.'

He goes on to explain that the Palace 'wines and dines' tabloid press journalists, hoping to furnish a better relationship with them and so avoid being torn to shreds in hostile news articles. He suggests that, regarding the Royal Family, *'I think everyone needs to have some compassion for . . . for them in that situation, right? There is a level of control by fear that has existed for generations.'*

So, according to Prince Harry, the British newspapers, at least the tabloid popular variety, holds the Royal family in a sort of grip of terror in case the press turns hostile. He is correct in this view: the 'gutter' press, as the tabloids are sometimes called by the people they attack, can play a prominent role in ousting politicians, prime ministers and even a king, in the case of Edward VIII.

Harry, however, has overlooked that the younger half of the United Kingdom (and world) no longer get their news, information or gossip from newspapers (nor even their online versions) any more. What, every Royal Personage should hold in terror in not the newspaper, or its online versions, but the ubiquitous buzzing phones that we all carry in our pockets or bags. These, when placed reverently upon our desks, or held in our hands to be studied for hour after hour every day, are the conduits of the mostly deadly threat of all, namely the 'social media.' A newspaper might sell a few hundred thousand copies these days, but the following chart shows how Instagram, Facebook and WhatsApp and the other channels dwarf all other means of conveying information:

Platform	World Users	UK users
Facebook	2.7 billion	51.34million
You Tube	2 billion	49.9million
WhatsApp	2 billion	34.7 million
Instagram	1.6 billion	27.2 million
Tik Tok	689 million	16.7 million
Snapchat	433million	14.1 million

Reddit	**430 million**	**7.5 million**
Pinterest	**416 million**	**6.7 million**
Twitter	**433 million**	**5.6 million**
LinkedIn	**310million**	**4.75 million**

The first three alone have a combined total of almost 7 billion worldwide users as of 2022, with 135 million of them in the U.K. We talk of social media and its messages and ideas going viral, but flashing through the ethernet *like lightning* might be a better analogy as microwaves send information that arrives virtually instantly – and lightning can both illuminate in a dazzling light, but also destroy those struck by too much of its awesome and overwhelming power.

CHAPTER NINE:
WHAT SOCIAL MEDIA TELLS US – SEISMIC SHIFTS BEFORE THE BIG EARTHQUAKE?

When Prince Harry talked of an invisible contract between the Royal Family and tabloid newspapers, he was only partially correct. Newspapers like the British dailies The Star, The Sun, Daily Mirror, Daily Mail and Daily Express don't feel 'contracted' or obliged to report good things about the Royal Family just because the Palace invites them for a cheese and wine party where a few snippets of positive gossip are dispensed along with the oer d'oeuvres. Nor do a few tame photo-opportunities of a smiling monarch, or of William and Kate parading their neatly turned-out children prevent tabloid journalists reporting anything critical of the Royals.

At these press conferences the journalists are merely put *temporarily* in a good mood. Rest assured, as soon as they leave Buckingham Palace, if even a minor Royal is seen committing an indiscretion (having an affair, breaking a law, being tipsy at a race meeting, swearing in public, sunbathing topless) then the chase is on. Anything remotely newsworthy will be hyped up into a boldly-headlined story 'in the public interest'. Yes, you can be sure no quarter will be given by ruthless tabloid hacks and the madding paparazzi. Princess Diana was literally hounded to death by the hacks chasing her limousine in 1997, and, despite numerous legal or non-legal attempts to control the worst excesses of swarms of royal reporters and photographers, not much has changed since then.

Though sales of paper copies of the tabloids and broadsheets have declined, their online versions have rocketed in popularity. Tens of millions of people read online newspapers and magazines every day. It is therefore unsurprising how many threads of conversation on the various social media platforms are sparked off by stories being broken by the big newspapers websites. For example on 29 January 2022 the Daily Express' online version ran the story:

HARRY AND MEGHAN'S £18M SPOTIFY DEAL UNDER THREAT IN NEW ANTI-VAX ROW

Almost immediately, that is, within minutes of the story emerging, twitter was awash with conversations such as

Mr E Mann @MrEMann9
Get your story right @Daily Express. Spotify have hired producers to kick ginge & cringes ass because they signed a deal and have only produced 1 podcast in the last 12 months. Typical #MeghanMarkle wanting the $ without working for it.

The twitter thread then runs and runs, fed and re-stimulated every few tweets by the Express itself. This is a bog-standard example of tabloid-inspired tweets both initiating and generating comment (about 75% of which, incidentally, are critical of Prince Harry and Meghan Markle).

The other tabloids all have similar threads; and each tweet similarly gives rise to more comments, re-tweets, likes, and downloads. The Daily Mail for example, using its MAIL+ online platform tweets a few hours later:

73

Mail+ @mailplus

Have Spotify lost patience with Prince Harry's podcast? And it's DENY DENY DENY from the Duke as Andrew comes out swinging. Our experts debate ALL the latest royal dramas in #PalaceConfidential @jo elvin @RE Daily mail @richardeden @KateMansey (2 retweets, 2 quote tweets, 23 likes). 29 Jan 22

What is interesting is the interaction between the news outlets as one reacts to another's breaking stories, the input often being made by quite senior journalists (or assistants working on their behalf) and the intertwining of 'tweeters' passing on, adding to, liking or downloading or replying. Of course, all this activity is generated in the name of spreading the news, which is partially at least a form of entertainment. But for those at the sharp end of its criticism and barbed gossip it can lead to painful and dangerous exposure – notice how Prince Andrew's name appears in the Mail+ tweet after a snippet about Prince Harry's podcast.

A less frantic but equally influential form of social interaction comes in the form of You Tube video consumption and its long strings of comments that accompany each film. Consider the film:

'Catastrophe for Prince Andrew and the Royal Family/ Palace Confidential' – You Tube (24,619 views within 6 hours)

In this film we see a news story about Prince Andrew which was first posted on the day it was announced in the USA that Prince Andrew must stand trial for alleged crimes against Virginia Giuffre. The film is basically a discussion between a journalist and a Daily Mail editor. It emerged only hours after the paper published the story. Daily Mail editor-in-chief Rebecca English

74

who was also an active tweeter of this subject matter (as well as contributing to the aforementioned tweets concerning Prince Harry) is seen answering questions about the prince's bold declaration that he was now 'demanding' a trial in the US. She explains the irony of Prince Andrew first seeking to dismiss Virginia Giuffre's civil case, but then seeming to relish the prospect of a battle in court (though in fact he had been *compelled* to go to trial).

What we see here on the You Tube is a rapidly generated broadcast from a journalist with her finger on the pulse of a royal story. Though the 'Mail' is generally considered pro-royalist, this social media version of the story does not hesitate to convey information that casts Prince Andrew in a poor light. The video content reveals Rebecca English being rather bemused by the prince's earlier strategy of denying many of Virginia Giuffre's accusations, and goes on to describe how Andrew's fall from grace as a working Royal might mean he has to pay for his own security in the future.

All very interesting – but it is the public's reaction, as expressed in comments below the video, that is even more fascinating. Within six hours 24,000+ views, and 170 comments had been generated. Of the 170 posts, three were neutral or supportive of Prince Andrew, 167 were critical, and about a third of the latter *strongly* hostile.

Here three fairly typical comments:

 teprakp
This is what can happen if a child is 'spoiled rotten' and totally indulged from birth. (36 likes)

Arel Ito

Royalty is about entitlement. So what can you expect but a bunch of power hungry, undisciplined and morally corrupt individuals who expect to live off others and get off scot free? The fact that some have carried out their duties diligently is only the exception not the rule....excuse the pun! (58 likes)

Markmark Mark

Andrew has used his body guards as golf ball collectors when he practiced golf In Buckingham palace. (16 likes)

Kate B

Clever Andrew forgets Maxwell. Maxwell, sitting in lockup, doesn't take Andy forgetting her well & becomes a surprise witness in exchange for a lesser sentence...

Clearly, the public are in an angry mood. It is most often the case that a video denigrating a royal person and depicting 'bad' conduct receives negative comments. The pattern is that posts condemning and vilifying the subject of a film cause many more to jump on the bandwagon. It often happens that the comments grow steadily more hostile as the criticism grows in volume, and we see a sort of 'pubic stoning by comment' effect. Occasionally there is a dissenter with a contrary view, but then the thread of harsh criticism resumes and the stream of negativity is off again.

Unfortunately for him, these days Prince Andrew attracts largely hostile social media interactions, and his humiliation by this incessant public pillorying is intensifying. If his mode of response is to hide away from the public's gaze, it is probably a wise one. These accumulating threads of criticism are impossible to reverse: there is no case yet of a person being pilloried online to the point of being 'cancelled' and then finding their way back into public acceptance. The online public are both brutal and relentless in their attacks on those perceived to have 'sinned', and their memory is long.

Therefore, a critical news story, a tweet or an online video might have dire and long-lasting repercussions for a celebrity, a Royal, or an ordinary citizen for that matter. And the accumulative effect of several forms of media creating conversations that branch into more and more threads can create the 'viral' reach of technology-enhanced news dissemination. In this way, critical information about an individual can spread and find its way into the consciousness of a population with frightening rapidity

You Tube, with its billions of users is an interesting platform in terms of its influence on people. Because it is seen mainly as a source of entertainment, viewers return again and again to their favourite topics – such as news of the Royal Family. And with so many negative stories emerging from Buckingham Palace in recent years, one wonders whether a tipping point has been reached. Instead of hearing mainly life-enhancing snippets of royal social engagements, diplomatic meetings and encouraging messages to their subjects, the British are now treated to an incessant barrage of negativity. The Prince Andrew situation is perceived as the greatest scandal. Then there is Harry and Meghan feeling that the Royal Family's lack of support for them necessitated a move to the USA. King Charles, in the lead-up years to his becoming king was often lambasted for his eccentricity, and, more seriously, for his passion for writing letters to politicians to influence local and national government. The penning of letters of 'advice' did not go down well in Britain. Nor did the news that the police are investigating the possibility that a Saudi businessman received an honorary knighthood for a cash donation to one of Prince Charles' charities. And there are numerous other matters concerning the Royal Family that are creating unease and criticism online, such as the cost of jet and helicopter transport which are being used for what are perceived as trivial excursions such as attending rugby matches.

It has to be said, however, that with You Tube, while it seems to be a rule that its critical videos generate mostly negative content, there are those that baulk this trend and appear largely immune from adverse comment. The late Queen and Prince William fit into this category, as we shall see later.

King Charles, however, certainly does not. Consider the video – 'The Truth About Prince Charles' Relationship With Prince Andrew' 174, 085 views 27 Jan 22

In this film the material looks at the deteriorating relationship between the two brothers. It is by no means critical of Charles, but includes accounts of Andrew's behaviour over the years that the elder brother detested. At the time of writing, there were 155 positive comments about Charles, with 74 negative posts (of which 41 are very scathing to the point of being vitriolic). There were 5 comments of a positive nature directed at Andrew, and almost all the rest critical or heavily critical. There were even 3 comments mildly critical of the late Queen, for example:

The Queen was 'too busy WORKING to bring up Charles and

took 18 months off WORK to look after Andrew.' Don't be ridiculous. These people don't WORK the way real people do...
John L 7 likes

And some people thought the Queen was being let down by her children and grandchildren:

Jake A
Her Majesty has worked tirelessly for this country and its people and the good of the Commonwealth. After 70yrs of dedication to duty, she is seeing her life's work shadowed by the disgraceful behaviour of her second son... All whilst dealing with the demise of her life partner and main support HRH Prince Phillip.

But by far the majority express disgust and disdain at Prince Andrew, and how they think he is responsible for his own demise:

M L
Prince Andrew still does not understand that socializing with sexual predators is a problem. 25 likes

And another example has the same telling refrain of Andrew being the weak link in the Royal Family, plus sympathy for the queen:

Linda G
Personally I believe Andrew is guilty. Feel for the Queen in that most of us have relatives that have done things that we did

not agree with. We can't control other's decisions... Yes, I would take it to a jury trial. Just from what I know – just saying. I think I would find him guilty but no payoff financially. 11 likes

Note also, how King Charles himself (then he was *Prince* Charles, of course) is also singled out for criticism:

joy h
Charles is one to talk about lifestyle specifically in the Royal Family considering his behaviour before, during and after his romance and subsequent marriage to Diana... It is my belief he does not deserve to be king and the baton should be handed, on her Majesty's demise to William whom I believe will be a hands on King ably accompanied by his loving wife Catherine and Charles can continue with his 'saving the planet' mantra. 11 likes

Time and time again we see criticism of Charles for the way he treated Princess Diana. She died 25 years ago, and a huge section of the public have still not forgiven him for his perceived ill-treatment of her:

Liz R
He has been a mess for a long time, and really Charles has little to talk about, Charles had his own sex scandal which was a big part of the downfall. And Charles married the woman who broke our hearts for Diana.

Which brings us on to another perceived 'weak link' in the Royal family: Camilla Parker Bowles is a woman who never fails to elicit strong opinions among the British, and the majority of those opinions are not favourable. In the comments below the rather partisan YouTube video 'Things About Camilla Parker Bowles That Are Beyond Weird', in a string of posts the public lets rip':

Virginia C
How could he take to this unattractive woman over beautiful Diana?

Poor Camilla has received 87% negative comments, of which about 25% are scathing. For example:

Susan G
Both Camilla and Charles were well into blood sports. They both enjoyed hunting and before she married Charles she attended a bullfight. There was a newspaper article showing her grinning with glee as a bull was being hacked to death. This tells me all I need to know about her.

According to all forms of social media, 'Camilla Parker Bowles' is less popular with British citizens than one recent YouGov poll might lead us to believe. Although 45% admitted to 'liking' her, 42% of British people 'disliked' her, with 14% undecided. But a far higher percentage of British negative comments on You Tube videos suggest that, even allowing for the provocative and partisan nature of some films, she may have a much higher disapproval rate in reality. However, it is reasonable to deduce that a strongly pro or anti royal film or news item can sometimes sway public opinion in the form of comments rather easily.

This is shown in the short 15 minute YouTube film 'Prince Charles tells the BBC his Aston Martin runs on wine and cheese' - BBC News' It is in fact an extract from the longer BBC TV film 'Prince Charles and his battle for our planet', a respectful interview that allows the future king to air his views on a number of environmental matters. Charles, who had a YouGov 'like' rating of 60%, receives 90% approval for his interview talking about his views on the environment and how to help save the planet – though his solutions of putting solar panels on his barns and running his classic sports car on surplus white wine may not have been enormously helpful to world debate on climate change. Nevertheless, without Camilla coming into the equation, he does evoke a deal of goodwill:

2 Slaza

Wonderful interview, seems like a genuinely kind and intelligent man. It's funny that for a long time he was considered to be a bit crazy for his views on the climate but now he's been proven right.

gracie2400

What a beautiful idea of planting avenues of trees for everyone who died in the pandemic. I wasn't quite sure what I thought of Charles but it gives me a bit of hope for our next monarch and the future ahead. 41 likes

Stuart W

He is so right I totally agree with him and I'm no royalist. Great interview thank BBC.

Unsurprisingly, He also almost 100% approval and sympathy when in another video released the same day he talks about losing his father, the late Duke of Edinburgh.

However, in the YouTube film 'Prince Charles and Camilla Celebrate 15 Years of Marriage' posted only two days after the speech on the death of his father on 9/4/21, Charles and Camilla are pilloried in the comments section. Of the first 100 comments, there are seventy-two negative, only 25 positive ones wishing the couple well, and three neutral.

Note well, this was a 'Royal Family Channel' film, and not one of the 'Republic' movement's offerings. If you are in any doubt as to why Charles is here so castigated, read the following comments:

C R
Charles doesn't deserve Diana. Diana will remain in our hearts forever 1.4K likes 3 replies

my_universe
If only he had married her back when they had first me, it would have saved them and Diana from so much heartbreak and tragedy... 1.5K likes 18 replies

It is notable too, how many people have added their 'likes' or 'replied' to the comments, showing just how many people actually read the comments, and react to them, as the next comment shows too:

Sunni F

Anytime I see Camilla, I cannot help but think of the pain experienced by Diana and her words that there were three people in this marriage. Love may have won out, but the path there was the destruction of the life of a beautiful young woman. I cannot warm to either of them as a result.   747 likes 24 replies

There are scores and scores in this vein; many are from across the world, but British ones make up the majority, and the proportion expressing scorn for Charles (and Camilla) is significant. And nowhere are there more critical comments engendered than on the ungracious REPUBLIC videos, as we shall soon see...

CHAPTER TEN:
MORE BAD THAN GOOD – THE OMINOUS
UNDERCURRENTS OF PUBLIC OPINION

When we turn to a decidedly anti-royal YouTube video of 27 March 2020 'The Man Who Shouldn't Be King' (which has 274,233 views at the time of writing) the future king Charles receives 91% negative comments, and the British public comes out spitting feathers:

For example:

John G
The man who talks about saving the environment who maintains a love of private jets and helicopters. I've never been able to reconcile his views with any semblance of credibility.

Sometimes we see the expression of sympathy for the Queen, and criticism of Charles himself:

Ro8Tam
I am a republican. I believe that the queen genuinely has done the job, as she sees it, to the best of her abilities. But she is not appointed by god, that is ridiculous. When she passed away we should have consigned the lot of them to the history books. We should leave no throne unburned. 2 likes

And the last thing the Royal Family want is people thinking too deeply about the nature the British constitution and coming up with logical deductions such as in the next post:

Helen B

An excellent documentary. We badly need a democratically elected Head of State. To those who say they bring tourism to the country, have a look at France. One of the most visited tourist attractions in Europe is the Palace of Versailles, yet France hasn't had a monarchy since 1789. Also, if all the palaces weren't occupied, more people could see them, which would bring in more revenue. Be honest, do you really check whether a country has a monarchy before you book your holidays?

Evidently, provoking a serious debate and getting people to think about the British way of government may not end well for the Royals:

Kay S

I never cared one way or the other about the monarchy because the Queen did a good job but now I really believe Charles is far too political and entitled. We need a referendum on the constitution; I would vote to abolish monarchy and the House of Lords

There are dozens upon dozens of these thoughtful comments, many of them coming to the same conclusion as this gentleman:

Adrian R

I am for getting rid of the monarchy. When Elizabeth steps down or passes away. Normal working families are using food banks. Normal young family's can't get on the housing ladder.

How many people living hand to mouth dreading and unexpected bills. While our monarch and her family live such wealthy lives. With no embarrassment. No morals... no we don't need this expense and these people 160 likes

Off with their royal heads! It would appear that many people have an inkling, as expressed in the comment below, that we are nearing the end of an era, and that Charles may not be a suitable replacement –

Smiley
I believe we are seeing the beginning of the end. Elizabeth 2 was well aware. Diana Spencer said he wasn't fit to be King possibly for other reasons, but her words will ring through.

It is in some ways predictable that an anti-royal film should both attract viewers who do not want Charles (or William for that matter) to be king. But the majority of comments are from casual or curious viewers shocked by the film's content regarding Charles. Moreover, the information in the video, while uncomfortable viewing for the Royal Family, is a true account of the Prince of Wales' life, beliefs and behaviour. It is quite clear, that were mainstream British TV and radio channels, and the popular daily newspapers, to host some serious debates on the subject of establishing a republic, then things would begin to look a little ominous for the Royal Family.

However, they do have a few tricks left up their ermine sleeves: the late Queen was and is virtually untouchable, even on You Tube videos and comments, the public remain loathe to criticise her too much, rather as one is loathe to say anything nasty about a dear departed favourite granny. A survey of comments after films such as 'Queen Elizabeth Lives An Insanely Lavish Life' (YouTube 1,295,043 views, Oct 5, 2020) still cannot evoke much of a negative comment. These three are typical:

Martin C
It's incorrect to describe Buckingham Palace as home. It's more like the office. Windsor Castle is more like home. 443 likes 16 replies

Sabrina L
Of course she lives a lavish lifestyle she's literally the queen. 94 likes 4 replies

David B
She actually lives a very simple and noble life. All that stuff belongs to the Nation. Her life comes with a huge price. She doesn't have privacy as we do. Her entire life is on a schedule....3 years in advance. It is fully evident that this Dear Lady cares more about the people than She does about Herself. She's proven it over and over again. 79 likes 8 replies

But of course, the Queen was at her most popular after the Christmas speech, with 98% positive posts, of which roughly 70% are *very* reverent. If You Tube comments are to be believed, the House of Windsor was safe enough, while she was alive...

Which leads us to a future monarch, Prince William. In the

BBC film 'Prince William: I don't lie awake waiting to be king' (YouTube 28/12/21, 2,071,018 views) the public are given ample opportunity to be negative about a future king. However, William receives even greater reverence than his grandmother, with 98% positive and 2% neutral posts.

A couple of typical ones read:

Simon I

I found the interviewer to be openly rude and a bit illogical. He seemed to be implying that somehow Prince William was taking it easy in some way, but serving the people by flying a rescue helicopter is surely one of the most admirable, selfless and worthy jobs you could think of. It's not any less "Royal" than sitting in committees and opening new buildings etc.

Glynis R simply commented:
I admire and respect Prince William so much.

The question is, can a video putting him in a bad light persuade the public to turn on him? In the film 'The Shady Side Of Prince William No One Talks About' on YouTube aspects of his past life are dragged up, including former relationships and an alleged affair with a friend of Kate Middleton. The Duke and Duchess of Cambridge are also accused of breaching strict UK Covid lock-down laws, amongst other things. The video is designed to shock viewers with William's 'bad' behaviour, but, nevertheless we see a 96% positive comments response. How interesting that the public didn't turn on Prince William when given the chance for a public stoning.

Gail C's attitude was pretty typical:

Well, if what is shady about Prince William is being young, immature and confused and to come on the other side of that more mature, wiser and more stable, there is no shame here. I hope his younger brother comes on the other side of his trial of life as well. He could learn from his older brother. But, they are two different men and have to make their own choices.

This certainly bodes well for Prince William – at the moment – but it is debateable as to whether he can remain the golden child of the Royal Family forever, given that he has to lead a perfect, blameless life in the full glare of publicity and with a volatile British public ready to chuck rocks at him the second he does anything to spoil his spotless image. His team of advisors, and the Prince himself, might be saying at present 'so far, so good'.

But trouble is still afoot for our newly crowned King, as we shall see in the next chapter, and the stark reality of the spendthrift royal juggernaut might just be the thing that brings him down – even before he gets used to wearing that golden crown.

First, however, we need to take a long hard look at another weak link in the family. According to many observers, William's younger brother Prince Harry is already doing all manner of damage to his brother's chance of becoming king in due course. By moving away from England with his wife, he gave the Royal Family the ultimate snub. According to the interview Harry and Meghan Markle had with Oprah Winfrey, the couple found it impossible to live within the confines of royal life. Some members of the family were unsympathetic to the pressures they felt, and as stated earlier, it was said a *senior* royal asked what skin tone Meghan's baby would have.

All in all, the picture portrayed of royal life was extremely negative, and part of the problem seemed to stem from the senior advisors at Buckingham Palace, who were said to have listened to accounts of Meghan's deteriorating mental health, but then did nothing to help her. Surprisingly though, Meghan, Duchess of Sussex does not fare too well as regards receiving favourable and supportive messages on social media, as we shall see later.

The British public are split in their attitude to Harry. In days of old, Prince Harry was a popular lad, as when the public wept to see him aged 12, walking manfully behind his mother's coffin en route to her funeral. In later years he fought for Queen and country, serving as a helicopter co-pilot in Afghanistan, often being filmed on the ground cavorting with his fellow officers and squaddies, enduring many of the hardships of that arduous and tragic campaign. In those days, his popularity was unquestioned. It soared higher during his courtship of Meghan Markle, and in the immediate aftermath of their marriage.

Then something went badly wrong. Clearly, his young wife did not take easily to Palace life. Posts on social media were often highly critical of her. Some elements of the Royal Family did not warm to her either. For a variety of reasons, the young couple relocated to the western USA, and the prince's popularity nosedived. Why? He receives mainly negative social media comments, though not as many as his spouse. It is true to say their appeal to the British public fell during their last months in the United Kingdom. The British tabloids had a field day criticising Meghan in particular for supposedly not hitting it off with her sister-in-law, the Duchess of Cambridge, and for being unable to complete her royal duties without fuss or complaint. After all, how hard could it be just to perform a few social engagements each day in return for the life of... a princess?

Evidently, the couple had their reasons for wanting to quit England and relocate to the USA. But when they went public with their story on American TV's Oprah Winfrey on March 7th 2021 the reaction was extremely unfavourable. In the TV show *'Oprah Winfrey Interview with Prince Harry and Meghan Markle'* Oprah elicited information suggesting the couple had been harshly treated by the Royal Family in the United Kingdom, and how Meghan in particular had not been well supported to the point of feeling suicidal.

However, within minutes of the video version appearing on You Tube ('Oprah Winfrey Interview with Prince Harry and Meghan Markle – Full Interview, 1,192,842 views) folk on both sides of the Atlantic made it plain who they thought was to blame for the couple's woes:

Rebecca S-B
When Harry finally comes to his senses and divorces her, I wonder if he gets his hard earned titles back? I hope so.

Here is typical example from hundreds of similar ones:

andrya
I was rooting for them until this interview and that is when I completely turned around and gave my full support to the RF. How dare they!!!!

It is perhaps surprising that so many of the comments, both from the UK and the USA, have such low opinions of Meghan:

Lauren
She's that one wife your friend marries that everyone says behind closed doors "I give it 5 years" 39 likes

And:
T R
I've never seen this before and I honestly don't know if I can stomach it. I just want to see her tell all the lies. I'm 1 min in and I may have to stop it. She LITERALLY makes me feel nauseous. 3 likes

As for Harry himself, only about 10% of the posts are 'positive' for him, many making him out to be a victim of Meghan Markle controlling him or 'being used' as one viewer puts it:

tyrone w
I just feel sorry for Harry. when he finally realises he was being used. As the old saying goes don't burn too many bridges. 57 likes

The next post seems to think Harry is a fine gentleman who made a mistake going to the USA:

Paulo Luckyluke
My highest respects to a steadfast, no nonsense, unassuming, entertaining man with a real sense of duty and dignity. It's

always an immense shame when people of such quality disappear from among us. I salute you, dear Prince. 21 likes

Harry and Meghan's popularity as a couple plummeted after they reached the USA. After the Oprah Winfrey film there were 50 consecutive negative comment, before this supportive one:

Lia M
I love them....they are so inspiring.

Then, the barrage of negativity continued. But Harry *can* still garner positive support, as the following film shows. In the YouTube film 'An Afternoon with Prince Harry & James Corden' (27,429,948 views by Feb 26, 2021) we see a lighter side of Prince Harry, as he is transported across Los Angeles on an open topped bus and interviewed by the British actor and comedian. The down-to-earth Harry at one point asks a householder along the route if he could use her loo, much to her and his host's amusement. This frank and funny interview evoked a different response from the public:

Y R
Harry is so down to Earth. This was a fun episode to watch. 1K likes 9 replies

One Of You
First time I see Harry being Harry. He's so accommodating, polite, down to earth, and supportive. A true prince... lol. 718 likes 7 replies

It appears that though Harry's wife seems to attract many negative comments, Harry himself is well enough liked. It has to be asked: is there an element of misogyny going on here? Or racism? The way that the wife seems disliked, but the husband garners glowing approval is puzzling. One is reminded of how Camilla, after 15 years of marriage, is still not accepted wholeheartedly as a 'Queen Consort', even though the late Queen granted her permission to use the title.

The public can be very harsh in its judgment of royal personalities. There seems to be an expectation of perfect virtue and blameless character, and complete intolerance of any lapses in 'good' conduct. Virtually unregulated social media platforms attract messages and threads showing elements of misogyny, nationalism, and yes, perhaps even barely disguised racism in the case of Meghan Markle. Some have said there might be a kind of beauty competition going on; or that unhappy people search for 'righteous' causes to which they can attach their inner feelings of rage and bitterness.

Whatever the motives may be, it is undisputed how social media trends, like magma rising beneath the earth's surface, may sometimes erupt in an outpouring of admiration and approval, as was shown during and after the marriages of William and Kate, then Harry and Meghan. On the other hand, the subterranean tremors may lead to a massive volcanic explosion of hatred, disgust and righteous indignation as was the case during the Duke of York's misfortunes.

In the case of the latter, as we have seen, this former golden boy of the press and second son of the Queen has now been reduced to a popularity rating of only 2%. Even if Prince Andrew had stood up to fight it out in court and won, it is difficult to see how he might have repaired his reputation. The online masses are unlikely to have believed a verdict favourable to him. Their minds were made up, rightly or wrongly, when the BBC Newsnight's first broadcast 'Prince Andrew & the Epstein Scandal: The Newsnight Interview'. This film was rapidly disseminated around the world. Later it was posted on You Tube as the notorious film 'Prince Andrew and the Epstein Scandal: The Newsnight Interview –BBC News.'

It soon became plain that, so far as the public are concerned, this interview was the real trial of Prince Andrew; and, unfortunately for him, he was found unanimously guilty by the public.

Proof of this is easy to find. Since its airing on November 2019 it has racked up 6.6 million views and thousands of comments – and *replies* to comments. Of the most recent 100, at the time of writing this, the posts are 97% negative. Only 1 of the last 100 comments is mildly supportive. A typical comment reads:

Martin T
Here's a man who is so accustomed to the magnitude of his position and his aristocratic pedigree intimidating those around him into subservience and silence, that he is completely unaware of how ludicrous he appears in this interview. His arrogance is so painfully evident at certain points, yet he thinks he appears gallant and composed. Thankfully he's medically incapable of perspiration.

There really is not much more to say about how the public perceive Prince Andrew, other than that his unpopularity is reflected on all channels of social media, and that *many comments made about him lead to negative aspersions being cast on the Royal Family in general.* It is quite possible, indeed probable, that the colossal weight of his misfortune may yet be enough to sink the whole of his family. The negative material pertaining to him posted on thousands of websites, and strung out in long threads on every social media platform is not going away anytime soon. Indeed, the threads are still lengthening.

Even cast out of most, but not all, of his roles, and with the majority of his titles stripped, he continues to hit the headlines for all the wrong reasons, for example by organising an expensive pheasant shoot just after being 'cancelled' by his own family. One wonders if he may yet suffer the fate of Edward VIII and be permanently exiled to Bermuda or France, now that the Queen, his erstwhile protector, has passed away.

But, even then, if Andrew were to disappear from the royal landscape, can the Royal Family recover its lost air of dignity, recoup its dwindling respect, or ever again be held in high esteem by a sceptical public who no longer believe in the myth of 'royalty'?

CHAPTER ELEVEN:
WHAT WHATSAPP AND FACEBOOK TELL US ABOUT THE ROYAL FAMILY'S FUTURE

On 24th January 2022 a WhatsUp open group conveyed a picture of the Queen and carried the following post:

'Anyone else getting a bit nervous about the Queen's health at age 95? I don't really care if she lives or dies, except I heard a rumour the other day that Charles is planning to use his army of connections to take over the government. Anyone else heard similar stuff?'

Rumours like this, however fantastical, often flit across the social media platforms, and for sheer speed and ease of use, nothing is quite as effective as a WhatsApp message. This platform is the most popular of the group messaging services, enabling connections to be made between more than two billion people worldwide. Often accused of misinformation spreading, even summonsing popular protests such as the Extinction Rebellion gatherings, it has been difficult to systematically study information flow on WhatsApp because of the semi-closed nature of some of the platform. What we do know, though, is that the perceived 'photogenic' nature of the Royal Family leads to a great deal of WhatsApp traffic pertaining to the Royal Family passing rapidly between royal watchers worldwide.

The potential danger is obvious: while WhatsApp may be used by 'fans', it can also be instrumental in 'cancelling' individuals by way of social media hate campaigns. Its messages are usually images sent with short, snappy parcels of information that make conveying a message to large audiences easy and instant, as in the following one, sent superimposed over an unflattering image of Prince Andrew's face:

Oh the grand old Duke of York
He had 12 million quid
He gave it to a girl he never met
For something he never did...

The use of groups of like-minded individuals means that messages and ideas can get more fervent, vehement and sometimes downright slanderous as individuals compete to contribute and say something 'punchy'. Certainly, there is a tendency for critical threads to ramp up in intensity. This is also a characteristic of Facebook groups, which though less rapid as a means of sending information to and fro, also generate 'conversational' threads with users commenting, replying and adding to topical debates.

One way for the Royal Family to try to improve their public image and encourage positive responses is by maintaining their own official Facebook pages. These typically offer attractive content that is both informative and unlikely to garner criticism. For example, the 'Charles, Prince of Wales' home page (now under a facelift as HRH's title changed to King Charles III) was a tasteful, well designed site with photographs, a letter congratulating the Queen on reaching her 70th year on the throne, and a friendly message to the public from Charles and his wife. You would think that everybody would be grateful upon reading this carefully thought out attempt at satisfying public curiosity. But no – directly underneath can be seen, on 24th February 2022 was the following post:

Lucy Mc
I'll never support these two. Have huge respect for our Queen No respect for them 2 likes 1 reply

To be fair, it has to be said that were very few other negative comments on this site. And the vast majority of those leaving messages on the new official King Charles III site are polite and thankful for the many photographs released there, or expressing condolences for his loss.

More varied comments are to be had (already) on the large unofficial 'open' groups set up by royal fans. These are where many thousands of individuals share information and offer opinions. Facebook, which is designed to get its users peering into its pages for as long as possible, must be delighted with the way its customers return daily to sites like these. This platform, with a worldwide reach of 2.7 billion people, is, of course, the digital forum of the world – which means it accommodates a full spectrum of viewpoints. There are, in fact, literally hundreds of royal fan group sites with pages focusing on royal matters, along with regular mainstream newspapers, magazines, TV channels and dedicated websites. Whichever way you look at it, the Royal Family are a big draw on this platform, and a mighty subject of gossip for individuals chatting to one another. Already, though, King Charles III is receiving some adverse comments such as this one referring to Prince Harry's new book about the Royal Family:

'Harry's book won't tell us any more than we already know about the King. He is far from perfect, has child tantrums and behaves like a spoiled brat...' MK, ('Charles III' site)

On another public group site we may read:

'According to my friend from Scotland Queen Elizabeth ruined the married life of King Charles to Princess Diana because Diana was a big threat to her' MM ('King Charles' Facebook page)

But, as is to be expected, King Charles gets mainly sympathetic posts on these heavily pro-Royal sites at this time so soon after the death of his mother. The fact that it isn't rosy and hospitable for him all the time, as a new king, and amongst his supposed fans is a little ominous. It is as if the public is waiting for him to do something 'bad' that they can latch onto as gossip.

Bad news certainly travels fast on facebook. One example of this will suffice to prove the point. On the UK's 'ITN' (International Television News) Facebook pages on 31 January 2022 the headline on its home page declared: 'Judge seeks High Court help with evidence about Prince Andrew from ex-assistant in sex assault case'. This ITV news report broke the story of how Virginia Giuffre's lawyers requested that Robert Olney, Prince Andrew's former equerry, should come forward for questioning prior to the trial scheduled for later in 2022. Below this page a thread of over a hundred comments sprang up in a matter of minutes. A head of steam similarly built up on the 'Prince Andrew Fan Club' site, as visitors trolled these pages even though the founders had politely headed the home page with the solemn notice in capitals:

THIS IS A FAN PAGE FOR THE DUKE OF YORK WE WILL NOT TOLERATE ANY NEGATIVITY HERE. HE DENIED THE ALLEGATIONS SO LET'S ALL JUST MOVE ON AND APPRECIATE THE WONDERFUL MAN HE IS

Here we see many posts still sympathetic to the prince, but the news headline above prompted a number of hateful messages, most of them not even mentioning the latest developments in the saga, such as this one posted on 22 January 2022:

MS   'No one ever should have to go through what his victims did! Being a royal doesn't stop you from preying and/or raping/forcing children regardless of age into sexual acts'   161 comments 16 likes

Clearly the warning notice placed at the top of the posts column has had no deterrent effect, as the next from 'Nathan' reads:

'If you genuinely have even an ounce of sympathy for Andrew, please take a good look in the mirror and ask what is wrong with you. Also, the victim blaming I've seen is absolutely disgusting.' 23 comments 16 likes

It would appear that, despite the best efforts of some, there is no safe haven where Prince Andrew's supporters can converse about him without somebody butting in with a hateful comment. The infiltration of this staunchly pro-royal site is an illustration of how web surfers in their billions, in particular those using facebook, are numerous and ingenious enough to find and inhabit all corners of the digital world. Elsewhere on Facebook there are even several examples of a 'Prince Andrew Jokes Page' and a 'Prince Andrew Memes Page'. These have rather more visitors to their sites than the fan sites. A video spoof of the song 'It wasn't Me' with unflattering images of the prince clocked 1.9 million views on one of the jokes pages. As stated earlier, the 'cancel culture' of our times is a ruthless, relentless and irreversible phenomenon.

As we have seen, King Charles currently gets mainly favourable posts on the many King Charles and Royal Family pages. On his old 'Prince of Wales' site there were quite a few (about 10%) critical grouches aired by non-fans on the numerous fan group sites leading up to his accession as king; but overall the gossip was pretty polite and focused on the pleasant pictures and good deeds he is photographed performing. Camilla, however, as on You Tube, can only expect a few positive comments before somebody pipes up with an adverse post, such as this by penned by 'Trevor' (and, incidentally, posted before 'The Crown' was aired on Netflix):

'A queen should be the example of all the good , of decency of moral, I don't' think it's quite right to name as queen a woman who has committed adultery and famously was the mistress, besides the king is the head of the English church. 2 likes

And this was on the mainly flattering 'Camilla Duchess of Cornwall should be Queen' site, as was 'Diana OK's viewpoint:

'I thought at one time, that they were going to bypass prince Charlie, for the throne and just give it to Prince William...no I do not think she should be queen...I think she could have handled herself differently when Diana was alive...Diana was only 19 when she married...Camilla was an adult...Why did Charlie do what he did any way... took advantage of Diana.....NO NO NO NO Camilla not for QUEEN'

And as for Harry and Meghan, the interest in them is mostly very supportive and reverent, with just the occasional one in ten or so having a snipe at their happiness, like 'JC' here:

'Harry, your wedding to Meghan could be the worst decision of your life'

As we have already seen, Facebook users seem intent on infiltrating even the most fervent and adoring fan sites and expressing their viewpoint. But what does the treatment of royalty on Facebook tell us overall about the public's current views on the various members of the family? Certainly, that there are hordes of royal watchers who receive each press release and piece of news with obvious relish; but equally well, there are those who cannot stop themselves expressing their strong views on the 'bad' behaviour of the Royals.

Examples of the latter include Charles' and Camilla's affair while both were still married, and the effect it had on Princess Diana; Prince Harry and Meghan Markle's disappointing exit from Great Britain, and her controversial Oprah Winfrey interview, widely held to be disingenuous. But the elephant in the Palace drawing room, remains Prince Andrew's alleged behaviour when consorting with Ghislaine Maxwell and Jeffrey Epstein.

Here we have come full circle – it was Ghislaine Maxwell and Jeffrey Epstein who first infiltrated the royal family through their association with Prince Andrew. Thus was the shell of the royal vessel, like that of Titanic, pierced with a deadly blow. And it could be argued that the icy water of public criticism has continued to flood into the sinking ship ever since then.

But is the good ship Windsor really sinking? What is the true magnitude and effect of Prince Andrew's scandalous shame on a seemingly firm institution which is over a thousand years old, and so far largely unchallenged? The Queen was revered. The slightly odd but good-natured Charles has ascended the throne; and after him comes the well-liked and quietly thoughtful Prince William. The latter is almost as well thought-of as the Queen herself. Surely such an old but deeply-rooted institution as the British Royal Family cannot fail after so prolonged a period of ruling the nation... can it?

CHAPTER TWELVE:
WHY THE HOUSE OF WINDSOR
WILL ULTIMATELY FALL

The accession of Charles, and the grief, pomp and ceremony surrounding the death of Queen Elizabeth II has focused attention on the role of the Royal Family like never before.

But, following the state funeral of a great queen, and the dying down of a nation's lamentations over its loss, the United Kingdom is faced with the stark reality of a new era. The late Queen was the very symbol and anchor of stability. Now that she has departed, it is inevitable that a great clamour for change will come. Young people in particular, will not long stand a new king sitting atop a hierarchy based on a social system of aristocracy that is by its very nature inegalitarian, undemocratic and rooted in the injustice of an outdated class system that denies opportunities to those not born into it. As the poll in chapter one shows, only 13% of *young* people in the UK thought Charles should become king, an astonishing statistic.

Also, it is patently absurd to believe that political stability and continuity requires an eccentric and quirky King Charles III to 'reign over' a populace still deemed 'subjects' by the terminology of an outdated British legal system. Where is the common sense, the justice, the logic, in transferring all the old archaic values – last carried by the late Queen who was born in British Empire and colonial times – to a new king crowned in a modern age?

Alas, the signs are already too clear. For a Royal Family *in its present form* to survive is not only unlikely, it is impossible. Criticism is coming from a broader base of disenchanted Britons, and growing in its intensity and clamour for change.

How can we be sure of this? While some of the anti-royal sentiment seems merely hateful and unfocused, the majority of voices have some valid and relevant criticisms to air. Organisations like 'Republic' have been very articulate in their criticisms of the Royal Family, and some of their reasoning is included below. However, for the most part, the evidence for the following four 'problems' of the Royal Family have been gleaned from social media sites and posts, news and magazine publications.

There is also information presented which has been gathered from various surveys – and among these is the one conducted by YouGov in 2022 that indicated, amongst other things, that *47% of Scots now want their country to become independent.*

The Welsh people, like the Scottish, also have a huge swathe of their citizenry demanding independence. YouGov discovered that, in a future referendum 23% said they would vote for independence, while 16% said they did not know. [Source: YouGov, October 2020] 13 seats are currently held by Plaid Cymru out of 60 in the Welsh Assembly. More ominously for the pro-royal, pro-Britain faction, a poll by 2020 YouGov found that 43% of Welsh 18 to 24 year-olds supported independence. Clearly, this does not bode well for the future of the Royal family, and explains why so much attention was paid by Buckingham Palace to Scottish and Welsh sentiment during the mourning arrangements of the late Queen.

Too bad that Buckingham Palace did not include Northern

Ireland to the same extent, where 42% declared they would vote to be part of a united Ireland, with 9% saying they did not know. Crucially, those wishing for a united Ireland include those of protestant as well as Catholic background, again with many young people looking to leave behind the old order of the British Crown ruling over Ulster.

There are four main problems with royalty that the younger generations of Great Britain cannot, and will not allow indefinitely.

These may be summarised as:

1. The problem of an unelected, immovable 'leader'
2. The problem of a monarch who meddles in affairs of state
3. The problem of waste and the squandering of resources
4. Secrecy: the big cover-up that hides the real truth

1.The problem of an unelected, immovable leader

The office of 'King' in twenty-first century Britain has become absurd, untenable and contrary to good democratic government. The late Queen's life spanned almost a century, and her sovereignty brought the United Kingdom from the time of a slowly crumbling Empire to the age of rapid, digitally-fast change and social revolution. Statues get knocked down by angry mobs of WOKE young people, university lectures are forced from office for adverse comments made about the new world of gender egalitarianism. The Queen's favourite son Prince Andrew was once the golden child of the family; war-hero and heart-throb bachelor, superficially a less boring contrast to the dour and stand-offish Charles – until the Duke of York was weighed in the scales of public opinion, and found wanting. Yet he remained in his royal posts and occupations for nigh on twenty years after he first became friendly with Jeffrey Epstein. Despite the press picking up on possible misdeeds, Andrew remained in his privileged position, even serving as a Counsellor of State after his disgrace over the Epstein affair, and after Charles succeeded their mother as monarch.

The difficulty here is that Royal Family members are born into public office and service, and cannot simply be voted out and replaced by better candidates. The stark reality is that the very privilege that they inherit makes them eminently unsuitable as leaders of military regiments, or charities, or universities, or organisations devised to help and protect the underprivileged in a western democracy. And in the matter of charities that require money for good causes, should members of the Royal family concern themselves with righting the wrongs of an inegalitarian society when their conspicuous over-consumption makes them a part of the problem, not a means of its remedy?

With Charles now king, his opinions, his pet projects and downright odd viewpoints are likely to continue to be projected and conveyed to those elected to power. But the public will not stand for this. Like his brother, he is in danger of finding himself 'cancelled'. Why? Quite simply, because he is unsuited to the task. If the job of 'King of the United Kingdom' came up, and the people of Great Britain were interviewing a thousand candidates, Prince Charles would, in all probability, be rather low on the list – perhaps even last.

The veteran political broadcaster, writer and commentator Andrew Marr said in an interview with the Daily Mail on 18 January 2022 that Prince Charles and Prince William intended to 'orchestrate a clear-out' in order to try to keep public opinion favourable to the idea of an unelected monarch. *'There is a sense that the whole issue of the future has not been discussed for a very long time,'* he stated. But with the Queen gone, he writes, the country will experience *'an ethical earthquake'*. As he put it: *'I do not think it is fully understood or appreciated how this is going to be an absolutely massive moment in all our lives. It will shake the whole country in a way that will be hard to explain until we actually live through it'*. He has no faith in Charles' attempts at reforming the monarchy. He said that *'the modern monarchy under Charles has to earn its place every day, every week and every month in people's affections.'* Marr has no doubts where the problem really lies: *'Some members of the royal family have been behaving like free riders. They assume the monarchy, the institution itself, can never be questioned. But the reason it is not being questioned was because of the Queen herself.'*

There is an ominous resonance to his predictions. The first tremors of the earthquake he mentions have already happened. Prince Andrew has been humbled. Prince Harry and his wife have caused a rift in the Royal Family. And yet the majority of the House of Windsor remains in situ. Even Andrew still has his royal residences and sufficient money to fund his lifestyle. There is no way that Charles will escape criticism and blame for the sorry state of the Royal Family today. The Queen was seen as the grandmother of the nation, untouchable and worthy of our trust. But Charles will not be able to bask in her glory when she is gone, and as soon as the mourning is over, the rumbles of cancellation will begin – right below the new king's feet.

2. <u>The problem of a monarch who meddles in affairs of state</u>
Charles' has broken protocol innumerable times by writing to politicians and government heads of department. But with the Queen no longer on the throne, the new king will be seen as an obstruction to progress, not a means of reform. Charles is the very epitome of the problem. He is said to have made questionable interventions on matters of architecture, town planning and even military matters. He wrote hundreds of letters every year which might adversely affect political decision making in Westminster and Whitehall. Clearly, the prince is no intellectual, his judgement is only that of one man outside the departments he seeks to influence. If he continues this behaviour, rest assured, the public will latch on to his meddling, and bring to bear the one thing Buckingham Palace cannot withstand: highly critical public opinion.

Do the British people really think this man has anything of value to contribute to intellectual debate? When there are 24 royal residences with the heating full on (Buckingham Palace alone costs upwards of *three million pounds* to heat and light), do we really need him telling the British public how to save the planet by running his Aston Martin, as he says, on white wine? When the full spectrum of media light illuminates this strange fellow, he certainly *will* be cancelled.

3. <u>The problem of waste and the squandering of resources</u>
This issue alone is enough to rouse the people of the United Kingdom into a frenzy. When the whole country is trying to recover from a covid epidemic, rampant inflation, a doubling in the cost of domestic energy, the last thing we want to see is a bunch of Royals in top hats going to the races or a rugby game

111

in a helicopter.

But what exactly do we mean by waste? The institution of royalty is an insane waste of public finances, an insane waste of the world's precious resources, and an insane waste of time for the hundreds of servants and lackeys tied into meaningless servitude for a largely idle and thriftless extended family that regards ordinary people as inferior 'subjects' to be humoured, or manipulated into a mode of servile flattery so that their own comfortable status quo may be maintained.

There are twenty-four royal residences ranging in size from gigantic to merely large and luxurious, with most of their rooms heated and for the most part, left empty! And how many are actually used even *in part* on a day to day basis? Furthermore, even if taxpayers money wasn't involved is it ethical that huge amounts of fuel is burned to heat and light such huge spaces when hard-working families are struggling just to pay their power bills? Pensioners are dying of cold for want of a few pounds to pay for gas and electricity to keep warm. Meanwhile, as I write this, Buckingham Palace's 600 windows are all illuminated, the heating is on full, and the King is snug in Windsor Castle.

Perhaps £3 million for heating and light is a drop in the ocean for the Royal Family. Let's hope one of the Palace's 1,000 servants remembers to switch off the lights and heat in the unoccupied rooms amongst the Palace's 775 high-ceilinged rooms and 79 corridors and landings. What a carbon footprint! What a terrible example to us all.

4. The problem of secrecy

With such spendthrift behaviour, it is no wonder Buckingham

Palace goes out of its way to keep its finances secret. It has been estimated[16] that the Royal Family receives £345m a year from the public purse. Financial secrecy and obscuring the true amounts paid by the taxpayer is actually *essential*, from the Royal Family's point of view, because if the public really focussed on the where its hard-earned money went, it would likely rebel instantly.

Helicopter trips to Scotland for shooting parties, or to Kent for Golf, or to polo matches have been observed. Charles once took a helicopter ride of 125 miles to a conference on air travel emissions in Cambridge.

As regards places to live, members of the Royal Family have plenty of choice in the matter of where they choose to reside. There are 24 royal residences. And while some of the stately piles listed below are privately owned, the fact that the royal family pays no death duties or inheritance tax gives them a huge (some would say unjust) advantage over the rest of the population.

The properties are:

Residence/ location/ occupant/ crown or privately owned

1. **Buckingham Palace (London) The King (CROWN) (Estimated £3m to power)**

2. **Windsor Castle (Berkshire) The King (CROWN) (£1m to power)**

3. **Palace of Holyroodhouse (Scotland) The King (CROWN)**

4. **Hillsborough Castle (Northern Ireland) The King (CROWN)**

5. **Sandringham House (Norfolk) The King (PRIVATE)**

6. Balmoral (Scotland) The King (PRIVATE)

7. Craigowen (Scotland) The King (PRIVATE)

8. Clarence House (London) The King (CROWN)

9. Highgrove (Gloucestershire) William/Kate (DUCHY OF CORNWALL)

10. Llwynywermod (Wales) William/Kate (DUCHY OF CORNWALL)

11. Tamarisk (Scilly Isles) William/Kate (DUCHY OF CORNWALL)

12. Birkhall (Scotland) King Charles (PRIVATE)

13. Kensington Palace (London) Prince William, the Duke of Gloucester, Prince and Princess Michael of Kent (CROWN)

14. Frogmore Cottage (Windsor) Princess Eugenie, Jack Brooksbank (CROWN)

15. Ivy Cottage (London) Princess Eugenie (CROWN)

16. Bagshot Park (Surrey) The Earl and Countess of Wessex (CROWN)

17. Royal Lodge (Windsor) The Duke of York, Princess Beatrice, Princess Eugenie (CROWN)

18. St James's Palace (London) Princess Anne, Princess Beatrice, Princess Alexandra, Lady Ogilvy (CROWN)

19. Wren Park (London) The Duke and Duchess of Kent (CROWN)

20. Thatched house Lodge (London) Princess Alexandra, The Honourable Lady Ogilvy (CROWN)

21. Anmer Hall (Norfolk) Prince William and family (PRIVATE)

22. Gatcombe Park (Gloucestershire) Princess Anne (PRIVATE)

23. Barnwell Manor (Northants) The Duke and Duchess of Gloucester (PRIVATE)

24. Adelaide Cottage (Windsor) William/Kate (CROWN)

As stated Buckingham Palace alone has 775rooms, with 78 bathrooms. There are roughly 100 toilets in the palace, with none of the latter available to the public when the parts of the building are thronged with tourists on its open days! Furthermore, Buckingham Palace toilets and bathrooms are strictly segregated between royalty and servants, and all palace staff are fully conversant of where they may go and where they may not.

And on that bizarre note, it is only left now for you the reader to retire and consider deeply whether the monarchy is likely to prevail, in one form or another, or if the people of the United Kingdom choose a better, more modern constitution to take it forward in the twenty-first century. At least, as Andrew Marr predicts, be prepared for the first steps into real change, be prepared for a sharp curtailing of the number of Royals living off the state, and a critical eye being cast on the more unacceptable practices of royalty. Then, the change urged on and led by the younger generations of Britons, the House of Windsor may finally be stood down as an unelected ruling elite asserting itself over the true governors of the country, that is, the ordinary voters.

Royalty approval and the sufferance of monarchs and their expensive families in the modern world rely on bluff, mystique, reverence and public approbation. But these airy nothings, like mist over the lawns of Buckingham Palace, can vanish in a trice.

Indeed, it can be argued, after looking at the present undercurrents of social media, that hostility, irreverence and public indignation at the excesses and transgressions of the Royal Family show that the time of reckoning has already come.

As one commenter on a YouTube royal video puts it:

'Royal Family? Unelected 'leaders? 'It's just a short matter of time before the whole sorry clan of shirkers, idlers and resource-wasting freeloaders is exorcised forever and a more democratic, accountable and logical system of governance is finally adopted.[17]

****

Review this book!

Whatever your views on the Royal Family, don't forget to leave a review of this book, where you can air your views on the way the British Monarchy is going. Go right ahead, YOUR opinion is important and I guarantee I'll be reading every word that you post.

– *Best wishes, Roland Gough.*

APPENDIX 1.

PRINCE ANDREW NEWSNIGHT INTERVIEW: TRANSCRIPT IN FULL RUN THROUGH LIE DETECTOR VSO SOFTWARE

This YouTube film 'Prince Andrew & the Epstein Scandal: The Newsnight Interview' was first broadcast on BBC Two on 16 November 2019.

The computer program uses VSO (Voice Stress Analysis) to attempt to detect patterns of speech that indicate possible lies.

PLEASE NOTE: Though the software manufacturers claim a high degree of accuracy in detecting lies and inconsistencies in spoken testimony, the author is makes no claim that the results of the software are either genuine proof of truth or falsehood. Indeed, the software writers recommend that the analysis should be taken as a means of 'entertainment' and not clear proof of falsehoods.

All indications of voice stress indicating possible lies are UNDERLINED. Some mannerisms and facial expressions are noted in bold type.

A full transcript of the BBC NEWSNIGHT interview of 17.11.19.

Emily Maitlis, interviewer: Your Royal Highness, we've come to Buckingham Place in highly unusual circumstances. Normally, we'd be discussing your work, your duty and we'll come on to that but today you've chosen to speak out for the first time. Why have you decided to talk now?

Prince Andrew: Because there is no good time to talk about Mr Epstein and all things associated and we've been talking to Newsnight for about six months about doing something around the work that I was doing and unfortunately we've just not been able to fit it into either your schedule or my schedule until *[BLINK BLINK = NERVOUS/UNDER PRESSURE]* now. And actually it's a very good opportunity and I'm delighted to be able to see you today.

MAITLIS: As you say, all of this goes back to your friendship with Jeffrey Epstein, *[HERE ANDREW WINCES/BLINKS RAPIDLY]* how did you first become friends? How did you meet?

ANDREW: *[LICKS LIPS WITH FEAR/BLINKS RAPIDLY]* Well, I met through his girlfriend back in 1999 who... and I'd known her since she was at university in the UK and it would be, to some extent, a stretch to say that as it were we were close friends. I mean we were friends because of other people and I had a lot of opportunity to go to the United States but I didn't have much time with him. I suppose I saw him once or twice a year, perhaps maybe maximum of three times a year and quite often if I was in the United States and doing things and if he wasn't there, he would say "well, why don't you come and use my houses?" so I said "that's very kind, thank you very much indeed". But it would be a considerable stretch to say that he was *[NOD NOD/ PAINED EXPRESSION]* a very, very close friend. But he had the most extraordinary ability to bring extraordinary people together and that's the bit that I remember as going to the dinner parties where you would meet academics, politicians, people from the United Nations, I mean

118

it was a cosmopolitan group of what I would describe as US eminents.

MAITLIS: Was that his appeal then?

ANDREW: Yes. *[HERE HE SHAKES HEAD AS IF MEANING 'NO']*

MAITLIS: Was that what you... because you were perceived by the public as being the party prince, was that something you shared?

ANDREW: Well, I think that's also a bit of a stretch. I don't know why I've collected that title because I don't... I never have really partied. I was single for quite a long time in the early 80s but then after I got married I was very happy and I've never really felt the need to go and party and certainly going to Jeffrey's was not about partying, absolutely not.

MAITLIS: You said you weren't very good friends but would you describe him as a good friend, did you trust him?

ANDREW: Yes, I think I probably did *[SHAKE OF HEAD AS IF SAYING 'NO']* but again, I mean I don't go into a friendship looking for the wrong thing, if you understand what I mean. I'm an engaging person, I want to be able to engage, I want to find out, I want to learn and so you have to remember that I was transitioning out of the navy at the time and in the transition I wanted to find out more about what was going on because in the navy it's a pretty isolated business because you're out at sea the whole time and I was going to become the special representative for international trade and investment.

So I wanted to know more about what was going on in the international business world and so that was another reason for going there. And the opportunities that I had to go to Wall

119

Street and other places to learn whilst I was there were absolutely vital.

MAITLIS: He was your guest as well, in 2000 Epstein was a guest at Windsor Castle and at Sandringham, he was brought right into the heart of the Royal Family at your invitation.

ANDREW: But certainly at my invitation, not at the Royal Family's invitation but remember that it was his girlfriend that was the key element in this. He was the, as it were, plus one, to some extent in that aspect.

MAITLIS: Am I right in thinking you threw a birthday party for Epstein's girlfriend, Ghislaine Maxwell at Sandringham?

ANDREW: Umm, no, it was a shooting weekend.

MAITLIS: A shooting weekend.

ANDREW: Just a straightforward, a straightforward shooting weekend.

MAITLIS: But during these times that he was a guest at Windsor Castle, at Sandringham, the shooting weekend...

ANDREW: Yeah, yeah.

MAITLIS: We now know that he was and had been procuring young girls for sex trafficking.

ANDREW: We now know that, at the time there was no indication to me or anybody else that that was what he was doing and certainly when I saw him either in the United States... oh no when I saw him in the United States or when I was staying in his houses in the United States, there was no indication, absolutely no indication. And if there was, you have to remember that at the time I was patron of the NSPCC's Full Stop campaign so I was close up with what was going on in those times about getting rid of abuse to children so I knew what the things were to look for but I never saw them.

MAITLIS: So you would have made that connection because you stayed with him, you were a visitor, a guest on many occasions at his homes and nothing struck you as suspicious...

ANDREW: <u>Nothing.</u>

MAITLIS: ...during that whole time.

ANDREW: <u>Nothing.</u>

MAITLIS: Just for the record, you've been on his private plane.

ANDREW: Yes.

MAITLIS: You've been to stay on his private island.

ANDREW: Yes.

MAITLIS: You've stayed at his home in Palm Beach.

ANDREW: Yes.

MAITLIS: You visited Ghislaine Maxwell's house in Belgravia in London.

ANDREW: Yes.

MAITLIS: So in 2006 in May an arrest warrant was issued for Epstein for sexual assault of a minor.

ANDREW: Yes.

MAITLIS: In July he was invited to Windsor Castle to your daughter, Princess Beatrice's 18th birthday, why would you do that?

ANDREW: <u>Because I was asking Ghislaine.</u> But even so, at the time I don't think I... certainly I wasn't aware when the invitation was issued what was going on in the United States and I wasn't aware until the media picked up on it because he never said anything about it.

MAITLIS: He never discussed with you the fact that an arrest warrant had been issued?

ANDREW: No.

MAITLIS: So he came to that Party knowing police were

investigating him.

ANDREW: Well I'm not quite sure, was it police? I don't know, you see, this is the problem, I really don't know.

MAITLIS: It was the Palm Beach Police at the time.

ANDREW: But I mean I'm afraid, you see this is the problem is that an awful lot of this was going on in the United States and I wasn't a Party to it and I knew nothing about it.

MAITLIS: In 2008 he was convicted of soliciting and procuring a minor for prostitution, he was jailed, this was your friend, how did you feel about it?

ANDREW: Well I ceased contact with him after I was aware that he was under investigation and that was later in 2006 and I wasn't in touch with him again until 2010. So just it was one of those things that somebody's going through that sort of thing well I'm terribly sorry I can't be... see you.

MAITLIS: So no contact?

ANDREW: No contact.

MAITLIS: When he was serving time there was no call, no letter, nothing there?

ANDREW: No, no, no.

MAITLIS: He was released in July; within months by December of 2010 you went to stay with him at his New York mansion, why? Why were you staying with a convicted sex offender?

ANDREW: Right, I have always... ever since this has happened and since this has become, as it were, public knowledge that I was there, I've questioned myself as to why did I go and what was I doing and was it the right thing to do? Now, I went there with the sole purpose of saying to him that because he had been convicted, it was inappropriate for us to be seen together. And I had a number of people counsel me in both directions, either to go and see him or not to go and see him and I took the judgement call that because this was serious and I felt that doing it over the telephone was the chicken's way of doing it. I had to go and see him and talk to him. And I went to see him and I was doing a number of other things in New York at the time and we had an opportunity to go for a walk in the park and that was the conversation coincidentally that was photographed which was when I said to him, I said, "Look, because of what has happened, I don't think it is appropriate that we should remain in contact," and by mutual agreement during that walk in the Park we decided that we would part company and I left, I think it was the next day and to this day I never had any contact with him from that day forward.

MAITLIS: What did he say when you told him that you were breaking up the friendship?

ANDREW: He was what I would describe as understanding, he didn't go into any great depth in the conversation about what I was... what he was doing, except to say that he'd accepted, whatever it was, a plea bargain, he'd served his time and he was carrying on with his life if you see what I mean and I said, "Yes but I'm afraid to say that that's as maybe but with all the attendant scrutiny on me then I don't think it is a wise thing to do."

MAITLIS: Who advised you then that it was a good idea to go and break up the friendship? Did that come from the Palace, was Her Majesty, the Queen involved?

ANDREW: <u>No, no, no, no, no, no, no, no, no, that came from...</u> <u>so there were a number of people who... so some people from</u> <u>my staff, some people from friends and family I was talking to</u> <u>and I took the decision that it was I had to show leadership and</u>

123

I had to go and see him and I had to tell him, "That's it."

MAITLIS: That was December of 2010.

ANDREW: Yep.

MAITLIS: He threw a Party to celebrate his release and you were invited as the guest of honour.

ANDREW: No, I didn't go. Oh, in 2010, there certainly wasn't a Party to celebrate his release in December because it was a small dinner Party, there were only eight or 10 of us I think at the dinner. If there was a Party then I'd know nothing about that.

MAITLIS: You were invited to that dinner as a guest of honour.

ANDREW: Well I was there so there was a dinner, I don't think it was quite as you might put it but yeah, OK I was there for... I was there at a dinner, yeah.

MAITLIS: I'm just trying to work this out because you said you went to break up the relationship and yet you stayed at that New York mansion several days. I'm wondering how long?

ANDREW: But I was doing a number of other things while I was there.

MAITLIS: But you were staying at the house...

ANDREW: Yes.

MAITLIS: ... of a convicted sex offender.

ANDREW: It was a convenient place to stay. I mean I've gone through this in my mind so many times. At the end of the day, with a benefit of all the hindsight that one can have, it was definitely the wrong thing to do. But at the time I felt it was the honourable and right thing to do and I admit fully that my judgement was probably coloured by my tendency to be too honourable but that's just the way it is.

MAITLIS: Because during that time, those few days, witnesses

124

say they saw many young girls coming and going at the time. There is video footage of Epstein accompanied by young girls and you were there staying in his house, catching up with friends.

ANDREW: I never... I mean if there were then I wasn't a Party to any of that. I never saw them. I mean you have to understand that his house, I described it more as almost as a railway station if you know what I mean in the sense that there were people coming in and out of that house all the time. What they were doing and why they were there I had nothing to do with. So I'm afraid I can't make any comment on that because I really don't know.

MAITLIS: Another guest was John Brockman, the literary agent. Now, he described seeing you there getting a foot massage from a young Russian woman, did that happen?

ANDREW: No.

MAITLIS: You're absolutely sure or you can't remember?

ANDREW: Yeah, I'm absolutely sure.

MAITLIS: So John Brockman's statement is false?

ANDREW: I wouldn't... I wouldn't... I don't know Mr Brockman so I don't know what he's talking about.

MAITLIS: But that definitely wasn't you getting a foot massage from a Russian girl in Jeffrey Epstein's house?

ANDREW: No.

MAITLIS: It might seem a funny way to break off a friendship, a four-day house Party of sorts with a dinner. It's an odd way to break up a friendship.

ANDREW: It's a difficult way of put... that's a very stark way of putting it, yes you're absolutely right. But actually the truth of it is that I actually only saw him for about, what the dinner

<u>Party, the walk in the Park and probably passing in the passage.</u>

MAITLIS: Let's go to that Central Park walk which was snapped. Friends of yours suggest that Epstein wanted that photo taken, perhaps he'd even set it up, do you worry that you were being played?

ANDREW: <u>Again, new information is coming out since his suicide has made us reappraise that walk in the Park.</u> We can't find any evidence or my staff and my people and I can't find any evidence to suggest that that was what he was doing. I mean you can look at it in so many different ways. The fact of the matter is is that somebody very cleverly took that photograph, <u>it wasn't as far as I remember nor do my security people remember, anybody being present or close because there were enough security around.</u>

<u>I mean there are even photographs of the security people who are around in the photograph. So I mean he could have done but...</u>

MAITLIS: Yeah, I guess what I'm asking is do you feel that you were Part of Epstein's public rehabilitation?

ANDREW: Oh no, funnily enough I don't, no. I mean if he was... if he was doing... if that photograph was taken with that purpose in mind, then it doesn't... it doesn't equate to what actually happened.

MAITLIS: So why wouldn't you announce this break up when you got that? Why wouldn't you publicly explain what you've done? Did you worry that he had something that could compromise you?

ANDREW: <u>No, no.</u>

MAITLIS: Do you regret that trip?

ANDREW: Yes.

MAITLIS: Do you regret the whole friendship with Epstein?

ANDREW: Now, still not and the reason being is that the people that I met and the opportunities that I was given to learn either by him or because of him were actually very useful. He himself not, as it were, as close as you might think, we weren't that close. So therefore I mean yes I would go and stay in his house but that was because of his girlfriend, not because of him.

MAITLIS: Was that visit, December of 2010 the only time you saw him after he was convicted?

ANDREW: Yes, yeah.

MAITLIS: Did you see him or speak to him again?

ANDREW: No.

MAITLIS: Never since then?

ANDREW: No, that was... funny enough, 2010 was it, that was it because I went... well first of all I wanted to make sure that if I was going to go and see him, I had to make sure that there was enough time between his release because it wasn't something that I was going into in a hurry but I had to go and see him, I had to go and see him, I had to talk.

MAITLIS: And stay with him, and stay in the house of a convicted sex offender?

ANDREW: I could easily have gone and stayed somewhere else but sheer convenience of being able to get a hold of the man was... I mean he was in and out all over the place. So getting him in one place for a period of time to actually have a long enough conversation to say look, these are the reasons why I'm not going to... and that happened on the walk.

MAITLIS: July of this year, Epstein was arrested on charges of sex trafficking and abusing dozens of underage girls. One of the

Epstein's accusers, Virginia Roberts...

ANDREW: Yeah.

MAITLIS: ... has made allegations against you. She says she met you in 2001, she says she dined with you, danced with you at Tramp Nightclub in London. She went on to have sex with you in a house in Belgravia belonging to Ghislaine Maxwell, your friend. Your response?

ANDREW: I have no recollection of ever meeting this lady, none whatsoever.

MAITLIS: You don't remember meeting her?

ANDREW: No.

MAITLIS: She says she met you in 2001, she dined with you, she danced with you, you bought her drinks, you were in Tramp Nightclub in London and she went on to have sex with you in a house in Belgravia belonging to Ghislaine Maxwell.

ANDREW: It didn't happen.

MAITLIS: Do you remember her?

ANDREW: No, I've no recollection of ever meeting her, I'm almost, in fact I'm convinced that I was never in Tramps with her. There are a number of things that are wrong with that story, one of which is that I don't know where the bar is in Tramps. I don't drink, I don't think I've ever bought a drink in Tramps whenever I was there.

MAITLIS: Do you remember dancing at Tramp?

ANDREW: No, that couldn't have happened because the date that's being suggested I was at home with the children.

MAITLIS: You know that you were at home with the children, was it a memorable night?

ANDREW: On that Particular day that we now understand is the date which is the 10th of March, I was at home, I was with the children and I'd taken Beatrice to a Pizza Express in Woking for a Party at I suppose sort of 4:00 or 5:00 in the afternoon. <u>And then because the duchess was away, we have a simple rule in the family that when one is away the other one is there.</u> I was on terminal leave at the time from the Royal Navy so therefore I was at home.

MAITLIS: Why would you remember that so specifically? Why would you remember a Pizza Express birthday and being at home?

ANDREW: Because going to Pizza Express in Woking is an unusual thing for me to do, a very unusual thing for me to do. I've never been... <u>I've only been to Woking a couple of times and I remember it weirdly distinctly. As soon as somebody reminded me of it, I went, "Oh yes, I remember that." But I have no recollection of ever meeting or being in the company or the presence.</u>

MAITLIS: So you're absolutely sure that you were at home on the 10th March?

ANDREW: <u>Yeah.</u>

MAITLIS: She was very specific about that night, she described dancing with you.

ANDREW: No.

MAITLIS: And you profusely sweating and that she went on to have a bath possibly.

ANDREW: <u>There's a slight problem with the sweating because I have a peculiar medical condition which is that I don't sweat or I didn't sweat at the time and that was... was it... yes, I didn't sweat at the time because I had suffered what I would describe as an overdose of adrenalin in the Falkland's War when I was shot at and I simply... it was almost impossible for me to sweat.</u>

129

And it's only because I have done a number of things in the recent past that I am starting to be able to do that again. So I'm afraid to say that there's a medical condition that says that I didn't do it so therefore... going to Pizza Express in Woking is an unusual thing for me to do'

MAITLIS: Is it possible that you met Virginia Roberts, dined with her, danced with her in Tramp, had sex with her on another date?

ANDREW: No.

MAITLIS: Do you remember meeting her at all?

ANDREW: No.

MAITLIS: Do you know you didn't meet her or do you just not remember meeting her?

ANDREW: No, I have... I don't know if I've met her but no, I have no recollection of meeting her.

MAITLIS: Because she was very specific, she described the dance that you had together in Tramp. She described meeting you, she was a 17-year-old girl meeting a senior member of the Royal Family.

ANDREW: It never happened.

MAITLIS: She provided a photo of the two of you together.

ANDREW: Yes, yes.

MAITLIS: Your arm was around her waist.

ANDREW: Yes.

MAITLIS: You've seen the photo.

ANDREW: I've seen the photograph.

MAITLIS: How do you explain that?

ANDREW: I can't because I don't... I have no... again I have absolutely no memory of that photograph ever being taken.

MAITLIS: Do you recognise yourself in the photo?

ANDREW: Yes, it's pretty difficult not to recognise yourself.

MAITLIS: Your friends suggested that the photo is fake.

ANDREW: I think it's... from the investigations that we've done, you can't prove whether or not that photograph is faked or not because it is a photograph of a photograph of a photograph. So it's very difficult to be able to prove it but I don't remember that photograph ever being taken.

MAITLIS: But it's possible that it was you with your arm around her waist?

ANDREW: That's me but whether that's my hand or whether that's the position I... but I don't... I have simply no recollection of the photograph ever being taken.

MAITLIS: The world has now seen the photo that Virginia Roberts provided taken by Epstein we understand in Ghislaine Maxwell's house.

ANDREW: Well here's the problem, I've never seen Epstein with a camera in my life.

MAITLIS: I think it was Virginia Roberts' camera, she said a little Kodak one that she lent to Epstein, he took a photo and your arm is round her waist.

ANDREW: Listen, I don't remember, I don't remember that photograph ever being taken. I don't remember going upstairs in the house because that photograph was taken upstairs and I am not entirely convinced that... I mean that is... that is what I would describe as me in that... in that picture but I can't... we can't be certain as to whether or not that's my hand on her whatever it is, left... left side.

MAITLIS: You think that...

ANDREW: Because I have no recollection of that photograph ever being taken.

MAITLIS: So why would somebody have put in another hand? You think it is next to her in the photo.

ANDREW: Oh it's definitely me, I mean that's a picture of me, it's not a picture of... I don't believe it's a picture of me in London because when I would go out to... when I go out in London, I wear a suit and a tie. That's what I would describe as... those are my travelling clothes if I'm going to go... if I'm going overseas. There's a... I've got plenty of photographs of me dressed in those sorts of... that sort of kit but not there.

MAITLIS: Just to clarify sorry, you think that photo has been faked?

ANDREW: Nobody can prove whether or not that photograph has been doctored but I don't recollect that photograph ever being taken.

MAITLIS: And you don't recollect having your hand...

ANDREW: No.

MAITLIS: ... round her waist in Ghislaine Maxwell's house on any occasion, even if it was a different date?

ANDREW: I'm terribly sorry but if I, as a member of the Royal Family, and I have a photograph taken and I take very, very few photographs, I am not one to, as it were, hug and public displays of affection are not something that I do. So that's the best explanation I can give you and I'm afraid to say that I don't believe that photograph was taken in the way that has been suggested.

MAITLIS: Why would people not believe that you were there?

ANDREW: I'm sorry, why would?

MAITLIS: I'm just trying to understand, there's a photo inside Ghislaine Maxwell's house, Ghislaine herself in the background, why would people not believe that you were there with her that night?

ANDREW: They might well wish to believe it but the photograph is taken upstairs and <u>I don't think I ever went upstairs in Ghislaine's house.</u>

MAITLIS: Are you sure of that?

ANDREW: Yeah, because the dining room and everything was on the ground floor, was as you came in... as you came in the hall. <u>So I don't remember ever going up there. I'm at a loss to explain this particular photograph. If the original was ever produced, then perhaps we might be able to solve it but I can't.</u>

MAITLIS: But you can say categorically that you don't recall meeting Virginia Roberts, dining with her?

ANDREW: <u>Yep.</u>

MAITLIS: Dancing with her at Tramp?

ANDREW: <u>Yep.</u>

MAITLIS: Or going on to have sex with her...

ANDREW: <u>Yes.</u>

MAITLIS: ...in a bedroom in a house in Belgravia?

ANDREW: <u>I can absolutely categorically tell you it never happened.</u>

MAITLIS: Do you recall any kind of sexual contact with Virginia Roberts then or any other time?

ANDREW: <u>None whatsoever.</u>

MAITLIS: Because she said in a legal deposition, a legal court document in 2015, she had sex with you three times. She is not confused about this. She said the first was in London when she was trafficked to you, the second was at Epstein's mansion in New York.

ANDREW: That is a date in April I believe, is that correct?

MAITLIS: She said it was a month or so later.

133

ANDREW: <u>Yeah, well I think that the date we have for that shows that I was in Boston or I was in New York the previous day and I was at a dinner for The Outward Bound Trust in New York and then I flew up to Boston the following day and then on the day that she says that this occurred, they'd already left to go the island before I got back from Boston. So I don't think that could have happened at all.</u>

MAITLIS: There was a witness there, Johanna Sjoberg who says that you did visit the house in that month.

ANDREW: <u>I probably did, on one of the weirder things, I was staying with the... because of what I was doing I was staying with the Consul General which is further down the street on the 5th so I wasn't... I wasn't staying there. I may have visited but no, definitely didn't, definitely, definitely no, no, no activity.</u>

MAITLIS: Because in a legal deposition 2015, she said she had sex with you three times. Once in a London house when she was trafficked to you in Maxwell's house.

ANDREW: Yes.

MAITLIS: Once in New York a month or so later at Epstein's mansion and once on his private island in a group of seven or eight other girls.

ANDREW: <u>No.</u>

MAITLIS: No to all of those?

ANDREW: <u>All of it, absolutely no to all of it.</u>

MAITLIS: Why would she be saying those things?

ANDREW: We wonder exactly the same but <u>I have no idea, absolutely no idea.</u>

MAITLIS: She made these claims in a US deposition.

ANDREW: Ummm hmmm.

MAITLIS: Are you saying you don't believe her, she's lying?

ANDREW: That's a very difficult thing to answer because I'm not in a position to know what she's trying to achieve <u>but I can tell you categorically I don't remember meeting her at all. I do not remember a photograph being taken and I've said consistently and frequently that we never had any sort of sexual contact whatever.</u>

MAITLIS: She spoke about you outside the court in August of this year? She said, I quote, "He knows exactly what he's done and I hope he comes clean about it."

ANDREW: <u>And the answer is nothing.</u>

MAITLIS: So if Virginia Roberts is watching this interview, what is your message to her?

ANDREW: I don't have a message for her because I have to have a thick skin. If somebody is going to make those sorts of allegations then I've got to have a thick skin and get on with it <u>but they never happened.</u>

MAITLIS: For the record, is there any way you could have had sex with that young woman or any young woman trafficked by Jeffrey Epstein in any of his residences?

ANDREW: No and without putting too fine a point on it, if you're a man it is a positive act to have sex with somebody. You have to have to take some sort of positive action and so therefore if you try to forget it's very difficult to try and forget a positive action and I do not remember anything. <u>I can't, I've wracked my brain and thinking oh... when the first allegations, when the allegations came out originally I went well that's a bit strange, I don't remember this and then I've been through it and through it and through it over and over and over again and no, nothing. It just never happened.</u>

135

MAITLIS: Epstein's housekeeper also in a Florida Court legal deposition said that you visited the Palm Beach residence around four times a year, you got a daily massage.

ANDREW: Four times a year?

MAITLIS: That was what he said in a Florida Court legal deposition.

ANDREW: No.

MAITLIS: I'm just wondering when you look back now, is there a chance that those massages might have been the services of someone who is being sexually exploited or trafficked by Epstein?

ANDREW: No, I don't think... I mean I... no, definitely not, definitely not and I definitely did not visit his Palm Beach house three of four times a year, absolutely not.

MAITLIS: How many times would you say you visited?

ANDREW: In total, probably four times in total throughout the time that I knew him. In fact probably that was the place that... if you see what I mean, he was in the house more there than in other... in other places that I was at.

MAITLIS: So that's where you'd find him?

ANDREW: But it was usually because I was going... I was going through and on somewhere else so it was a day, that was it.

MAITLIS: You said in your statement from the Palace, at no time did I see, witness or suspect any suspicious behaviour.

ANDREW: Yeah, yeah.

MAITLIS: Virginia Roberts's legal team says, "You could not spend time around Epstein and not know what was going on. You could not spend time around Epstein and not know what was going on."

ANDREW: If you are somebody like me then people behave in

136

a subtly different way. You wouldn't... first of all I'm not looking for it, that's the thing, you see, if you're looking for it, then you might have suspected now with the benefit of a huge amount of hindsight and a huge amount of analysis, you look back and you go well was that really the way that it was or was I looking at it the very wrong way? But you don't go into these places, you don't go to stay with people looking for that.

MAITLIS: "You could not spend time around him," that was what they said, "You could not spend time around him and not know".

ANDREW: The other aspect of this is that... is that I live in an institution at Buckingham Palace which has members of staff walking around all the time and I don't wish to appear grand but there were a lot of people who were walking around Jeffrey Epstein's house. As far as I was aware, they were staff, they were people that were working for him, doing things, I... as it were, I interacted with them if you will to say good morning, good afternoon but I didn't, if you see what I mean, interact with them in a way that was, you know what are you doing here, why are you here, what's going on?

MAITLIS: But you'd notice if there were hundreds of underage girls in Buckingham Palace wouldn't you?

ANDREW: Oh God, but sorry you would notice if there were hundreds of underage girls in Jeffrey's house. Wasn't there, not when I was there. Now he may have changed his behaviour patterns in order for that not to be obvious to me so I don't... I mean this is... you're asking me to speculate on things that I just don't know about.

MAITLIS: You seem utterly convinced you're telling the truth, would you be willing to testify or give a statement under oath if

137

you were asked?

ANDREW: Well I'm like everybody else and I will have to take all the legal advice that there was before I was to do that sort of thing. But if push came to shove and the legal advice was to do so, then I would be duty bound to do so.

MAITLIS: Because you've said there are many unanswered questions, everyone affected wants closure, you would help to provide that closure.

ANDREW: If there was... in the right circumstances, yes I would because I think there's just as much closure for me as there is for everybody else and undoubtedly some very strange and unpleasant activities have been going on. I'm afraid to say that I'm not the person who can shed light on it for a number of reasons, one of which is that I wasn't there long enough. And if you go in for a day, two days at a time, it's quite easy I'm led to believe for those sorts of people to hide their activities for that period of time and then carry on when they're not there.

MAITLIS: Virginia Roberts's lawyers, legal team say that they've asked for a legal statement from you. There is an active FBI investigation, would you be willing to provide that?

ANDREW: Again, I'm bound by what my legal advice is... legal advisers tell me.

MAITLIS: Epstein was found dead.

[Here Andrew smiles]

ANDREW: Yep.

MAITLIS: In prison.

ANDREW: Yes.

MAITLIS: In August of this year.

ANDREW: Yep.

MAITLIS: What was your response on hearing that he'd died?

138

ANDREW: Shock.

MAITLIS: Some people think that he didn't take his own life.

ANDREW: There again, I'm not one to be able to answer that question. I believe that centres around something to do with a bone in his neck so whether or not if you commit suicide that bone breaks or something. But I'm afraid to say I'm not an expert, I have to take what the coroner says and he has ruled that it was suicide so...

MAITLIS: He's dead, his girlfriend Ghislaine Maxwell, your old friend was, victims say, complicit in his behaviour.

ANDREW: That bit I can't help you with because I've no idea.

MAITLIS: Do you think that she has questions to answer about her role in this?

ANDREW: In the same way that I have questions to answer in the sense of what was I doing and as I say that I was there to... to my mind be honourable and say to him, "Look, you've been convicted, it would be incompatible for me to be seen with you," but unfortunately somebody was standing around with a camera at the time and got a photograph of us. It's one of the very few photographs there are of us but that was... that was the case.

If there are questions that Ghislaine has to answer, that's her problem I'm afraid, I'm not in a position to be able to comment one way or the other.

MAITLIS: When was your last contact with her?

ANDREW: It was earlier this year funnily enough in the summer, in the spring, summer.

MAITLIS: About what?

ANDREW: She was here doing some rally.

MAITLIS: So even though he had by then been arrested and was facing charges of sex trafficking?

ANDREW: <u>No, no, no, no, no, no, no, this was... this was early spring I think, it was long... because when was he arrested?</u>

MAITLIS: July.

ANDREW: <u>No, it was before July.</u>

MAITLIS: And that was the last time?

ANDREW: Yeah, yeah.

MAITLIS: Did you discuss Epstein at all?

ANDREW: <u>No, actually funnily enough no not at all, there wasn't anything to discuss about him because he wasn't in the news, you know, it was just... we had moved on.</u>

MAITLIS: I want to talk about moving on now.

ANDREW: Oh yeah, right, okay.

MAITLIS: Epstein is dead.

ANDREW: Yes. *[Here a flicker of a smile can be seen on Prince Andrew's lips]*

MAITLIS: The women are now being heard.

ANDREW: Quite rightly.

MAITLIS: How do you move on from this?

ANDREW: Well, it's an interesting way of putting it. I'm carrying on with what I do. I have a number of things that I have been doing since 2011, they're pretty well organised, pretty successful and so I'm carrying on and trying to improve those things that I'm already doing.

MAITLIS: I wonder what effect all this has had on your close family? You've got your daughters of your own.

ANDREW: It has been, what I would describe as a constant sore in the family. We all knew him and I think that if we have a conversation about it, it's... we are all left with the same thing, what on earth happened or how did he get to where he was,

140

what did he do, how did he do it? And so it's just a constant sort of gnaw. I mean this first came out in 2011 and it was a surprise to... to all of us because the photographs were published at a separate time to when I was there and then we sort of questioned what on earth is going on and as a family we discussed it. And then in 2015 when the allegations were made in the deposition, there was a sort of... there was a sort of... this is the immediate family, not the wider family. The wider family couldn't be more supportive but the immediate family, it was well, what's all this about? And we all just were at a loss so it's just...

MAITLIS: Has the episode been damaging to the Royal Family, to Her Majesty the Queen?

ANDREW: I don't believe it's been damaging to the Queen at all, it has to me and it's been a constant drip if you see what I mean in the background that people want to know. <u>If I was in a position to be able to answer all these questions in a way that gave sensible answers other than the ones that I have given that gave closure then I'd love it but I'm afraid I can't. I'm just not in a position to do so because I'm just as much in the dark as many people.</u>

MAITLIS: How do you reconnect with the public then now?

ANDREW: Exactly what I'm doing which is to use and to continue to work with Pitch, to continue to work with iDEA and the things that I believe strongly in. I'm not somebody who does things in competition with people oddly. I do things in collaboration with people. So I want people to... to work together to come to, as it were, a solution to a bigger problem. And so I got a number of people working together, particularly in the education field, Particularly in... and also in areas of government and what they are doing so that we're bringing everybody together so that we're all pushing in the same direction and iDEA now does that. We've been going properly now for two years, we've got 3.5 million people who got a badge. We've got half a million, or just over half a million young people are using the service and I'm trying to think what else we've got. But it's... well it's designed for seven to 14-year-olds in the United Kingdom and it turns out it's done from 5 to 95 around the world so it's being done in 100 countries now. So we're slightly on the catch-up at this point.

MAITLIS: I know we have to bring this to a close because we're running out of time. You've faced questions today on a very, very raw subject. There has never been an interview like this before, I wonder what that tells us about the way the Royal Family now confronts these difficult situations. Has there been a sea change?

ANDREW: I think the problem that I'm... we face in the 21st Century is social media. There is a whole range of things that you face now that you didn't face 25 years ago because it was just the print media. And I think that to some extent there is a... there is a thick skin that you have to have and again I'm not a confrontationist myself. I would prefer to be able to, as it were, resolve things in a way that is sensible. And so choosing to, as it were, get out there and talk about these things, it's almost... it's almost a mental health issue to some extent for me in the sense that it's been nagging at my mind for a great many years. I know that I made the wrong judgement and I made the wrong decision but I made the wrong decision and the wrong judgement I believe fundamentally for the right reasons which is to say to somebody "I'm not going to see you again" and in fact from that day forth, I was never in contact with him. The subsequent allegations are, what I would describe as surprising, shocking and a distraction. But that's... I mean there are all sorts of things that are on the internet and out there in the public domain that we just sort of go, "Well, yeah," but I'm afraid is... it just never happened.

MAITLIS: You've talked about a thick skin, I wonder if you have any sense now of guilt, regret or shame about any of your behaviour and your friendship with Epstein?

ANDREW: As far as Mr Epstein was concerned, it was the wrong decision to go and see him in 2010. As far as my association with him was concerned, it had some seriously beneficial outcomes in areas that have nothing and have nothing to do with what I would describe as what we're talking about today. On balance, could I have avoided ever meeting him? Probably not and that's because of my friendship with Ghislaine, it was... it was... it was inevitable that we would have come across each other. Do I regret the fact that he has quite obviously conducted himself in a manner unbecoming? Yes.

MAITLIS: Unbecoming? He was a sex offender.

ANDREW: Yeah, I'm sorry, I'm being polite, I mean in the sense that he was a sex offender. But no, was I right in having him as a friend? At the time, bearing in mind this was some years before he was accused of being a sex offender. I don't there was anything wrong then, the problem was the fact that once he had been convicted...

MAITLIS: You stayed with him.

ANDREW: I stayed with him and that's... that's... that's the bit that... that... that, as it were, I kick myself for on a daily basis because it was not something that was becoming of a member of the Royal Family and we try and uphold the highest standards and practices and I let the side down, simple as that.

MAITLIS: This interview has been exceptionally rare, you might not speak on this subject again, is there anything you feel has been left unsaid that you would like to say now?

ANDREW: No, I don't think so. I think you've probably dragged out most of what is required and <u>I'm truly grateful for the opportunity that you've given me to be able to discuss this with you.</u>

MAITLIS: Your Royal Highness, thank you.

ANDREW: Thank you very much indeed.

****

Review this book!

Whatever your views on the Royal Family, don't forget to leave a review of this book, where you can air your views on the way the British Monarchy is going. Go right ahead, YOUR opinion is important and I guarantee I'll be reading every word that you post, as will many others interested in the future role of royalty. Best wishes, Roland Gough.

LEGAL DISCLAIMER

The author wishes to make plain that he has simply compiled and assessed the opinions, statements, accusations, suggestions and data of reporters, investigators, legal authorities and other individuals and organisations in a discussion of the matter outlined in this book. There is no stating or suggestion that the allegations made against Prince Andrew or any other persons mentioned in this book are either true or false. That is solely a matter for others to decide.

REFERENCES

1. YouTube video comment, G ee: 'King Charles III a Modern Monarch', Sky News, 1/10/22.
2. The Telegraph 12/1/22
3. The Sun, The Times 30/1/22
4. Estimated
5. Real name withheld
6. Oxenberg, Christina. Trash: Encounters with Ghislaine Maxwell (p. 85). Independent Kindle Edition.
7. Ibid p91
8. Ibid p94
9. Attrib. Potter Stewart
10. The Sun
11. CTV News 5/5/21
12. AOL News 19/1/22
13. 6/6/22 West Newton, Norfolk
14. Interview
15. Interview
16. Estimated by Republic group
17. YouTube video: PG 'Insane Things King Charles III Demands of his Servants' 1.10.22

Printed in Great Britain
by Amazon

25812890R00086